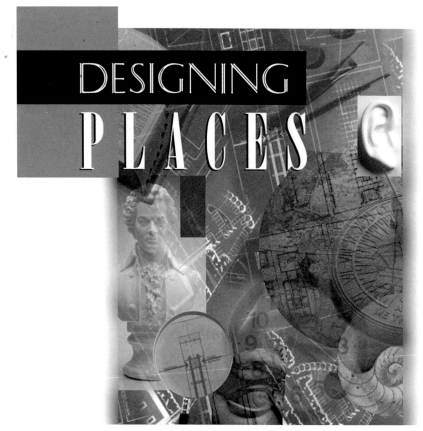

DESIGNING
PLACES

FOR LEARNING

ASCD

ASSOCIATION FOR SUPERVISION
AND CURRICULUM DEVELOPMENT

ALEXANDRIA, VIRGINIA

CEFPI

THE COUNCIL OF EDUCATIONAL
FACILITY PLANNERS, INTERNATIONAL

SCOTTSDALE, ARIZONA

EDITED BY ANNE MEEK

**Association for Supervision
and Curriculum Development**
1250 N. Pitt Street • Alexandria, Virginia 22314
Telephone: (703) 549-9110 • Fax: (703) 549-3891

Gene R. Carter, *Executive Director*
Ronald S. Brandt, *Director of Publications*
Nancy Modrak, *Managing Editor, ASCD Books*
Julie Houtz, *Senior Associate Editor*
Biz McMahon, *Assistant Editor*
Ginger Milller, *Copy Editor*
Gary Bloom, *Manager, Design and Production Services*
Stephanie A. Justen, *Print Production Coordinator*
Karen Monaco, *Senior Graphic Designer*

The Council of Educational Facility Planners, International
8687 E. Via de Ventura, Suite 311, Scottsdale, AZ 85258
Telephone: (602) 948-2337 • Fax: (602) 948-4420

Tony J. Wall, *Executive Director*
Deborah P. Moore, *Director of Administration*

From the Editors:
We welcome readers' comments on ASCD books and other publications. If
you would like to give us your opinion of this book or suggest topics for future
books, please write to ASCD, Managing Editor of Books, 1250 N. Pitt St.,
Alexandria, VA 22314.

ASCD Stock No. 1-95082
ISBN 0-87120-248-4

Library of Congress Cataloging-in-Publication Data
Designing places for learning / edited by Anne Meek.
     p.   cm.
    Includes bibliographical references.
    "ASCD Stock No. 1-95082."
    ISBN 0-87120-248-4
    1. School buildings—United States—Design and construction. 2. School
environment—United States. 3. Educational change—United States.
    I. Meek, Anne.
  LB3218.A1D47 1995
  371.62'0973—dc20   95-4409
                                        CIP

DESIGNING PLACES FOR LEARNING

FOR LEARNING

PREFACE

THE IMPORTANCE OF
THE SCHOOL AS PLACE

For 12 years you've heard the story. SATs are down, teachers can't teach, administrators are unnecessary, the economy is in a tailspin, America is losing its competitive
edge, we must evaluate teachers, make the school day longer, make the school year
longer, test students more, and cut out the frills. This line of reasoning has led to torrents
of finger-pointing rhetoric from policymakers and the press and a steady stream of
reforms, the positive effects of which go largely unnoticed by either the media or the
perpetrators of the rhetoric.

Imagine, then, my surprise upon hearing a different line of reasoning from Govern-
or Gaston Caperton of West Virginia when he spoke to the first National Conference on
Educational Facilities, sponsored by the Council for Educational Facilities Planning,
International, in Washington, D.C., in 1991. Governor Caperton's thinking went like this:

- West Virginia's people are undereducated and, therefore, less productive than they
  could be.
- West Virginia's schools are rundown and obsolete.
- Our citizens are not proud of these schools and feel no ownership for them; conse-
  quently, they do not value learning.

- If the people were proud of their schools and vested in them, they would value learning and their children would value learning, too. West Virginia would develop a highly skilled work force and then could compete successfully for better jobs and new industries in the global economy.
- Therefore, let us offer our limited state funds so localities can design and build new schools that will instill pride in the community and ensure productivity and a better life for all in West Virginia.

With this line of reasoning, Governor Caperton moved above and beyond the punishing rhetoric, declining to identify work force development as the primary purpose of schooling. Instead, he recognized the symbolic importance of the school as a place in the life of a community. That is, he took into account the nature of the human heart: what we value, what we attach importance to—that is what determines our ambition, effort, pride, and commitment.

After all, it's not easy for people to attach deep meaning—a sense of belonging, affection, and loyalty—to the index of leading economic indicators or to an economic development office in their state. But it *is* easy, in fact, inevitable, to attach deep meaning to the school where you first trudged up the steps to make friends and meet teachers; where, perhaps, you lost your first tooth or your heart for the first time or made your first touchdown; learned the difference between the teacher's rules for the playground and the real rules; played in the band; tried out for the senior play; understood the beauty of algebra or the chemistry of cooking; or began to see the connections between the Elizabethan origins of the settlers of your state and the language of your family.

What Governor Caperton has tapped is what the poets call *a sense of place* and what the social scientists call *a sense of community*. Both terms denote the symbolic importance we attach to the places we inhabit.

We are "coached" into these associations by vivid sensory impressions and innumerable interactions with others—except, of course, for those deep meanings that reside in the innate sensibilities called the collective unconscious. A school building, its playgrounds and playing fields, its bus lanes and bathrooms, is replete with coaching and interactions. And we inhabit schools when we are young and impressionable, when our minds are busy with the tasks and issues of deep meaning. For these two reasons, the school as a place is fertile ground for the creation of deep meaning and, therefore, of symbolic importance in the hearts and minds of the people.

This book illustrates ways of looking at schools as places of deep meaning and shows how that view of schools can alter our approaches to designing, constructing, and renovating the buildings we inhabit. I hope this book will encourage educators, policymakers, architects, and facilities planners to feel comfortable with a larger vision of the mission of schooling than work force development, and provide practical examples of concepts and strategies to achieve that larger vision by acknowledging the symbolic importance of the school as place.

—ANNE MEEK

SYSTEMIC SCHOOL REFORM: IMPLICATIONS FOR ARCHITECTURE

EDWARD B. FISKE

AMERICAN SCHOOL ARCHITECTURE IS AS DEEPLY ROOTED IN 19TH CENTURY VALUES AS EVERY OTHER ASPECT OF EDUCATION. THEREFORE, IF WE ARE TO SUCCESSFULLY REFORM THE SYSTEM OF PRIMARY AND SECONDARY EDUCATION, WE MUST GIVE SERIOUS THOUGHT TO THE DESIGN OF SCHOOLS AND THE OVERALL LEARNING ENVIRONMENT.

By any standards, the 1983 National Commission on Excellence in Education's report *A Nation at Risk* represented a major turning point in American public education. It pushed the quality of education onto the national political agenda, and goaded virtually every state legislature and state board of education in the nation into enacting some sort of program to improve primary and secondary education.

With the wisdom of hindsight, however, it is clear that the vision inherent in *A Nation at Risk* and its ensuing reform efforts were seriously deficient. The vision assumed that public schools in the United States could attain world-class standards by improving the schools as currently organized. Thus, the reforms of the mid- to late1980s concentrated on goals such as tighter curriculums, higher salaries, more rigorous certification standards for teachers, and more testing of students and teachers alike.

By the end of the last decade, however, it became clear that tinkering with the current system was not enough. The fundamental problems lay not with lack of money, rigor, or effort on the part of students or teachers, but with a system that has long outlived its usefulness. The system was based around familiar but now outmoded values such as centralized and hierarchical management and instruction based on what John Goodlad and others have dubbed "teacher talk." We have been trying to use a 19th century system of education to train 20th century youngsters to function in the 21st century, and it was never going to work. What we had to do was to go back and reorganize the system as a whole.

This is exactly what is now happening. Americans have begun rethinking and redesigning the most fundamental aspects of the way we run our schools—a process variously known as "restructuring" or "systemic reform." We are looking at every aspect of education, from the way we run districts, manage schools and classrooms, and organize time to how we test students, hold people accountable, and relate schools to the surrounding community. And we now know that an important element of this systemic reform concerns the physical structures of schools. American school architecture is as deeply rooted in 19th century values as every other aspect of education. Therefore, if we are to successfully reform the system of primary and secondary education, we must give serious thought to the design of schools and the overall learning environment.

Thus far, little discussion has taken place about the architectural implications of restructuring, which is hardly surprising. For one thing, there has been relatively little construction of new schools in recent years. And, more important, the design of restructured schools must reflect values and ideas that are only now beginning to attain any kind of public consensus.

Nevertheless, it is not too early to speculate about the contribution that architects can make to the systemic reform movement.

 SOME PRELIMINARY THOUGHTS ON THE SUBJECT

I first became aware of systemic reform in the late 1980s when, as Education Editor of the *New York Times*, I was traveling around the country writing about the spate of school reform efforts inspired by *A Nation at Risk*. After several years, I began to realize the sweeping nature of these reforms. Name any aspect of a public school system, and I had probably written a news story about someone who was doing it in a way that was breaking sharply with traditional practice. Put all the pieces together, and what you had was a rethinking and reworking of the entire system.

The problem was that no one had put all the pieces together. Some people were working on decentralizing administration, others on active learning for students, still others on new approaches to assessment and outcome-based accountability. But no one had taken the new approaches to learning and put them in a school with shared decision making in a district committed to new forms of assessment and accountability. It was like the old story of the blind men and the elephant. Each one had his hands on a piece of the elephant, but none of them had a concept of what the entire elephant was like.

THE PROBLEM WITH THIS NEW CHALLENGE IS THAT SCHOOLS ARE STILL ORGANIZED AROUND THE OLD "FACTORY" MODEL.

The fact that we have embarked on the restructuring of American public education should come as no surprise. Just about every other large institution in the developed world is going through similar systemic change—from large corporations to the American military and the health care system. All are finding that they must make radical adjustments to remain competitive and vigorous in today's fast-changing world.

In the case of public education, the imperative for fundamental change is readily apparent. Consider the conditions that existed when public education was organized in the late 19th and early 20th centuries. It was a time when plenty of people could and did get along quite well without a high school diploma. It was a time when those who did graduate from high school—only 6 percent of the population in 1906—needed little more than rudimentary literacy and numeracy skills; indeed, in the case of those working in the heavy industrial sector, the tasks were made as simple and repetitive as possible. And it was a time when you could get away with having only a minority of people—say a fifth to a quarter—do the thinking for the entire system.

We now live in a radically different world—one in which the educational stakes are much higher. Today, everyone needs a high school diploma, and most people need thinking skills. Take the mechanic in the local garage, for example. He can no longer get away with just looking and listening and kicking tires. He needs to know how to read complex manuals and use sophisticated diagnostic equipment, which is to say that he must operate at a new level of abstraction. This kind of upskilling is occurring in virtually all fields, blue- and white-collar alike. Preparing students to succeed in such a world places a whole new set of demands on our schools. We are asking schools to do for most students what in the past was required of only a few. We are asking them to teach everyone to think!

 ## MOVING AWAY FROM THE FACTORY MODEL

The problem with this new challenge is that schools are still organized around the old "factory" model. Authority is centralized and flows down from the top. Teachers, like workers along an assembly line, are seen as interchangeable parts, and students are viewed as products moving along an assembly line. As Albert Shanker of the American Federation of Teachers likes to describe it, we put them in a room, do something to them, ring a bell, put them in another room, do something to them, and so forth. Most classes are dominated by teacher talk, and an entire class of students typically follows the same rigid schedule. Accountability has virtually nothing to do with how much students learn; instead, it is tied to seat time for students and following the rules for teachers.

The structural revolution now under way in American public education seeks to change this by replacing the factory model system with one based on a whole new set of values. Indeed, each of the underlying values of the old system is being turned on its head.

- Centralization is giving way to decentralization. Local schools are gaining more autonomy from central boards, and are, in turn, bringing teachers, parents, and others into the decision-making process.
- Standardization is giving way to respect for diversity. We all know that students learn in different ways. Now we are building multiple teaching styles and respect for diverse learning styles into the system.
- Fixed time is giving way to defined academic performance as the basis for organizing instruction. Students are expected to attain certain levels of proficiency. Because some students need more time to meet these standards, ways are being found—computerized instruction, peer tutoring, summer school—to give them the added time.
- The longstanding focus on process is giving way to a preoccupation with results. No longer is it sufficient for teachers simply to present information and follow all the rules. Accountability for

teachers lies in what students know and are able to do after instruction.

Implicit in this new value system for schools are some very radical ideas, starting with new expectations about learning. We have now begun to assert that all children can learn at a relatively high level. In one sense, this notion is incontestable. With the exception of children with brain damage, every single child in an American school has already done the single most difficult thing that any human being ever does: learned a mother tongue. Yet, by the time children reach school age, we have come up with all sorts of reasons why some students—especially the poor, members of racial minorities, and other "at-risk" youngsters—cannot be expected to perform well in school.

National Standards

The push is on for national standards. The United States is unique among industrialized countries in that it has operated a decentralized system of education and has never held a national debate over what it expects schools to accomplish. However, the realities of the new global economic and political order are forcing U.S. citizens to acknowledge the collective stake that we have in the students this decentralized system produces. That's the underlying reason that education became a major national political issue in the 1980s, and it is the principal force that feeds the growing support among political and educational leaders to establish a national system of standards and assessments. This new awareness of a national stake in quality education does not mean that we are moving toward federal control of schools or even a national curriculum. What it means is that states and local school districts, while still free to run their own schools, will be judged on how their students perform against national standards.

New Roles for Teachers and Students

We are also building radical new ideas into the teaching and learning process. We have begun to demand that, instead of sitting passively and absorbing information, students must play an active role in their own learning. Theodore Sizer of Brown University argues quite correctly that under the factory model of schooling it was the teacher who did the real "work" in the classroom. But no one learns to think by sitting in a passive mode and receiving information. One learns to think by learning how to generate information and then manipulate what one has obtained. Under the new model of active learning, the student is the "worker," and the role of the teacher is that of a "coach" who oversees the student's self-learning process. This transformation of roles, though, requires that teachers be regarded as competent professionals who come to their task with a fund of pedagogical and subject knowledge and are capable of making independent judgments about how to manage the educational process.

Put all of these changes and radical ideas together, and you have nothing less than an entirely new concept of education—a concept that focuses not on teaching, but on learning. Education is not about transferring information from the head of a teacher into the head of a student. Education in an information society means equipping students with the ability to think. To put it another way, education is "learning to learn."

In sum, what we're talking about is a systemic, or structural, revolution based on a whole new concept of education and a whole new set of values. It's a revolution that is well under way, but still proceeding in fits and starts, piece by piece. What will count in the final analysis is how the various pieces—the parts of the elephant, if you will—fit together. No one knows exactly how this will happen or what the elephant will look like. Indeed, the importance of diversity means that there probably will not be a single elephant but many varieties suitable to different situations.

ARCHITECTURE'S ROLE IN THE TRANSFORMATION OF EDUCATION

What does all this mean for the architecture of schools? The question is an important one because systemic reform demands by definition the rethinking of all aspects of the structure of schooling, including the design of school buildings and other physical aspects of the learning environment. You cannot decentralize the management of schools or transform pedagogy without giving thought to the physical context in which these activities will take place. Similarly, architecture must be informed by the new values and goals of education.

As with the rest of the systemic reform movement, it's difficult to predict at this time what the architecture of restructured schools will look like. It is possible, however, to identify some broad ideas and themes that are likely to influence the architecture of restructured schools.

Work Space for Students

The traditional notion of the classroom is that of an enclosed public space in which the teacher, standing at one end, can readily address a group of students. Such a design, of course, stems directly from the idea that education centers on what the teacher does and says.

The new concept of teacher as "coach" and student as "worker" demands a different approach. Thinking about design must start with the needs of the learners, not of the teacher. Thus, the classroom must be thought of not as a public space for communication between the teacher and a group of students but as a collection of work stations. Students must be provided not with a simple chair and desk facing the teacher but with personal working space that offers access to the various tools required to engage in serious learning, including computers and other new technologies. These work stations need not be elaborate or expensive, but the concept of a personalized working area as opposed to a piece of public space is important.

IF WE ARE SERIOUS ABOUT THE NOTION THAT AMERICAN TEACHERS ARE PROFESSION-ALS, THEN SCHOOLS MUST PROVIDE THEM WITH SPACE IN WHICH THEY CAN ENGAGE IN PROFESSIONAL ACTIVITIES.

The factory model school perceives learning as an individualized activity. Students are expected to work on their own, and collaboration with peers is viewed as cheating. This view contrasts sharply with the way teaching and learning occur in adult work places, where cooperative thinking and group accountability are now taken for granted. Educators are beginning to take note of such trends and to incorporate techniques such as peer tutoring and cooperative learning into schools. The new work stations of restructured schools must permit such activities.

Professional Space for Teachers

One of the first things that strikes the American visitor to a Japanese school is the teachers' room. In the United States, teachers typically have a lounge where they can eat lunch, grab a cup of coffee, and relax in each other's company. Everything from the soda machine to the overstuffed couch sends out the message that the function of the room is social rather than professional.

In Japan, the message is quite different. For one thing, there are often several teachers' rooms, one for math and science teachers, another for language arts and social studies teachers, and so forth. Each teacher has a desk, usually with access to a telephone for contacting students' parents. There is common space, but it is arranged so that it can be used not only for relaxation but for discussions of curriculum, lesson planning, and other professional matters. One reason for building such space into schools, of course, is that Japanese teachers spend less time in the classroom than their American counterparts. They are expected to spend several hours a day honing lessons and engaging in dialogue with their colleagues about how to improve instruction, and they need a place to do this.

If we are serious about the notion that American teachers are professionals, then schools must provide them with space in which they can engage in professional activities. This means that they need the basic tools of any professional—a desk and (hold onto your seats!) a telephone. They also need a place to discuss serious educational issues.

I was interested to see the newly created teachers' room in the Prairie School in Racine, Wisconsin. As with most American schools, public or private, the original designers made no provision for such a professional space, but the Prairie School teachers' room was recently carved out to accommodate new concepts of the teacher's role. Each teacher has a desk facing one of the four walls, and access to a telephone. For economic reasons, instead of a telephone on each desk, there is a single telephone with a 20-foot cord that can be

THE SYSTEMIC REFORM MOVEMENT MUST TAKE THIS TREND TOWARD SMALLER AND MORE PERSONAL LEARNING ENVIRONMENTS EVEN FURTHER.

moved from desk to desk. Not ideal—but an important first step.

Smallness of Scale

The new focus on student learning as opposed to public discourse by teachers means that school architects must think small. There must be provision for students to work together in small groups, and individual work stations aimed at encouraging higher-order thinking skills. Likewise, the new emphasis on respecting the diversity of student learning styles means that the overall instructional space should be divided up into a variety of smaller learning environments.

In response to a large body of research questioning the value of large schools, American educational planners have already begun taking steps such as dividing high schools into smaller "houses" or similar units with their own faculty and other resources. The systemic reform movement must take this trend toward smaller and more personal learning environments even further.

Invisible Technology

New technologies play an important role in restructuring American education, though not necessarily in obvious ways. Technology is value-neutral. Computers can be put in the hands of students and used as powerful tools for active learning, or they can remain under the control of teachers and become a vehicle for sophisticated teacher talk. School districts can distribute computerized budget systems to implement site-based management, or they can use them to give new meaning to micromanagement. It all depends on the values people bring to them.

Technologies geared to the new values of systemic reform will play a role in virtually every aspect of school restructuring. They are necessary tools for decentralizing management, transforming teachers into coaches and facilitators, making students active learners, and developing new forms of assessment. From an architectural point of view, this means that technology should not become a focus of attention in itself, as with a computer laboratory, but all-pervasive and thus invisible. Fish do not have a name for water.

Horizontal Communication

One of the defining characteristics of the factory model school was its emphasis on vertical communication. The centralization of authority meant that significant communication took place between superiors and inferiors—principal to teachers, teachers to students—rather than among peers. Thus, teachers, while reigning supreme behind the closed doors of their own classrooms, knew

SCHOOLS MUST PERMIT THE STUDENT, WHOSE PHYSICAL PRESENCE NOW DEFINES THE PLACE OF EDUCATION, TO MOVE EASILY FROM ONE LEARNING STATION TO ANOTHER.

little about what went on in the next classroom or on the next floor, much less in another school. From the point of view of school administrators, it meant trouble if teachers got together to discuss professional matters. Similarly, students were expected to sit and do their own work quietly, not to communicate with each other.

Systemic reform places great value on promoting horizontal as well as vertical communication. Students must learn to work in groups, and teachers, who are professionals, must engage in professional discourse. Architects must keep this priority in mind when designing walls, windows, and hallways, locating administrative offices, and establishing electronic-mail systems.

Openness to the Outside

The structural revolution in American elementary and secondary education raises the questions: What is the *place* of education? Where does education occur?

In the past the answer was simple. Education occurred in the classroom where the teacher dispensed knowledge and students gathered to take it in. According to the new definition of education, however, the location of the teacher becomes less important than the location of the students. The teacher is the coach of the learning process, and coaching can take place in a variety of venues. Students can learn from teachers and libraries in the school building, but they can also use modems to connect to satellites and other sources of outside databases, and they can do so from virtually anywhere, including their homes.

The architectural consequences of this new concept of the place of education are considerable. Whereas up to now schools have been organized around the sanctity of well-defined learning spaces—self-contained classes protected from the noise and distractions of hallways and other classrooms—they must now open themselves up. They must permit the student, whose physical presence now defines the place of education, to move easily from one learning station to another. They must provide places, physical as well as symbolic, where students can access external databases.

Other ways schools must express openness include a redefinition of the relationship between the school and the community. Traditional school architecture literally places walls between the school and the outside environment. There is nothing about it that says "Welcome." The new concepts of school-based management and shared decision making, however, seek to build close ties between the school and community. Thus, they require an architecture with windows, doors, and other design features that invite traffic.

Perhaps an analogy to higher education would be useful.

I have always been struck by the difference in feeling between the central campuses of Harvard and Stanford Universities. Harvard Yard is a wonderful, intimate space. As you stroll through it, you can almost hear the voices of William James and Henry David Thoreau and others who have lived there in the past echoing in your ears. It inspires contemplation. On the other hand, the courtyards of the central campus of Stanford, which took its inspiration from newer American institutions rather than the great English and European institutions of the late Middle Ages, are spacious and airy. They exude openness. They push the mind toward thoughts about future possibilities rather than achievements of the past. The architecture of restructured primary and secondary schools must be more Stanford than Harvard.

Flexibility

If only for economic reasons, school design has always emphasized flexibility. Gymnasiums double as auditoriums, and audiovisual equipment is put on wheels so it can be moved about the school. In thinking about the architecture of restructured schools, it's important to maintain and develop this principle of flexibility because systemic reform is not a goal so much as a continuing process. You cannot talk about a restructured school—only about a restructuring school. We still don't know what the "elephant" will look like, and from an architectural point of view we must keep our options open.

After serving for slightly more than a year as president of Yale University, the late A. Bartlett Giamatti was asked what he missed most about being a regular member of the faculty. He replied without hesitation: the opportunity to "stalk" ideas. The deepest joy of the academic life, he said, was to pose a question and then go into the library and follow whatever leads presented themselves. New technologies have opened up virtually unlimited opportunities to stalk information and ideas, but schools must be organized so as to encourage such sleuthing. This means students must have ready access to a variety of media—books, electronic encyclopedias, modems, and so forth—and they must be able to move easily from one to the other.

· · ·

As noted at the outset, the thinking through of the architectural consequences of restructured primary and secondary schools in this country has only begun. I conclude by offering two brief thoughts on how this process might best proceed. First, it's important that the architecture of restructured schools flow from the new values and concepts—active and student-centered learning, teachers as professionals, and so forth—that undergird the systemic reform movement. Designs that spring from a formalistic architectural

ARCHITECTS NEED TO DEVELOP SOME INTERIM SOLUTIONS RATHER THAN HOLD OUT FOR RADICAL NEW DESIGNS.

perspective, however innovative, will probably not do the job.

Second, architects need to develop some interim solutions rather than hold out for radical new designs. For the foreseeable future, there will probably be far more opportunities to remodel existing schools than to build new ones from scratch.

Architects have a key role to play in the movement for systemic reform of American public schools. The design of physical structures offers an important means of giving concrete expression to abstract ideas, and new approaches to school design can themselves be an effective tool for communicating the new educational values. This is an exciting time for teachers, administrators, and policymakers to be part of education in the United States—watching the country drag its schools from the 19th into the 21st century. The same can be said of those who will be rethinking the physical structures as well.

THERE IS MOUNTING EVIDENCE
THAT MANY ARCHITECTURAL
CHARACTERISTICS OF SCHOOLS
CAN *AND DO* AFFECT
ATTITUDES, BEHAVIORS, AND
ACADEMIC ACHIEVEMENT.
SOME ARE DIRECT IMPACTS OF
BUILT FORM ON EDUCATION,
WHILE OTHERS ARE INDIRECT
LINKAGES BETWEEN ARCHITEC-
TURAL CHARACTERISTICS
AND INTERVENING
PSYCHOLOGICAL PROCESS. . . .

— GARY T. MOORE (1995)

DESIGN PATTERNS FOR AMERICAN SCHOOLS: RESPONDING TO THE REFORM MOVEMENT

2

GARY T. MOORE
AND JEFFERY A. LACKNEY

An elusive yet critically important relationship exists between architectural design and education reform. To compile a set of design *patterns* that respond to aspects of the current school reform movement in the United States, we reviewed empirical literature about the impact of the designed environment on educational performance (several dozen studies on the effects of environmental design on teacher attitudes and student attitudes, behavior, and achievement), architectural literature (looking at over 100 innovative educational facilities), and, especially, the education reform literature.

This review and synthesis of the literature led us to seek answers to questions such as these: Does the designed environment affect educational performance? How will shared decision making affect the physical layout of classrooms and whole school buildings?

Note: An earlier and longer version of this chapter was presented as a keynote address at the Prairie School National Conference on Architecture and Education, Prairie School and Wingspread Conference Center, Racine, Wisconsin, May 16, 1992. Our thanks to Henry Halsted and the Conference Planning Committee for their confidence and support. For the full report, *Educational Facilities for the 21st Century*, write: Center for Architecture and Urban Planning Research, University of Wisconsin–Milwaukee, P.O. Box 413, Milwaukee, WI 53201-0413.

LARGER SCHOOLS (WITH 1,000 OR MORE STUDENTS), DISCOURAGE A SENSE OF RESPONSIBILI- TY AND MEANINGFUL PARTICIPA- TION,

What are the implications of new forms of assessment, such as portfolios, on the use of classroom space? How will the process of furthering teacher professionalization affect the privacy needs of teachers? Are findings from the empirical literature reflected in recent design trends?

As we found answers to these and related questions, we created a set of 27 design patterns that respond to current reforms, including several that have been shown through empirical research to contribute to educational achievement. Several patterns identified here are based on the groundbreaking work of the California Department of Educ-ation (1990) in *Schools for the 21st Century* and the work of the Architectural League of New York (1992) in *New Schools for New York: Plans and Precedents for Small Schools.* The following seven sample patterns—(1) And the Winning School Is . . . Smaller, (2) The School as a Community Hub/Necklace of Community Activities, (3) Team Suites/Clusters of Classrooms, (4) Supervisable Circulation Paths, (5) Small Classrooms, (6) Portfolio Process Studios, and (7) Clusters of

Teacher Offices—provide an overview of our discoveries about the link between architecture and effective educational reform.[1]

AND THE WINNING SCHOOL IS . . . SMALLER

In addressing the issue of optimal overall size of school buildings, the Public Education Association (cited in District of Columbia Commission on Public Education 1989) recommended downsizing schools to 500 to 600 pupils based on the argument that smaller schools will lead to a more humane educational system. But what is the evidence?

Between the early 1960s and 1980, 344 articles were published pertaining to the effects of school size on academic achievement and other achievement-related variables. Prior to the '60s, many educators and policymakers believed that increasing the size of schools was an important reform idea, which led to comprehensive schools in Great Britain and regional schools in the United States. Larger schools were more cost-effective and believed to be more educationally efficient. In the now-classic *Big School, Small School,* ecological/environmental psychologists Roger Barker and Paul Gump

---

[1]Since that time, we and our students have developed a more comprehensive set of 50 patterns that respond to a wide range of education reforms. We hope these and a series of 12 prototypical designs will be available in a traveling exhibit.

(1964) conducted a study of very big (over 2,000 students) and very small (100–150 students) high schools in Kansas and concluded that small schools offered students greater opportunities to participate in extracurricular activities and to exercise leadership roles. In particular, participation in school activities, student satisfaction, number of classes taken, community employment, and participation in social organizations were all superior in small schools relative to large schools.

A review of some of the subsequent studies by James Barbarino, which appeared in an article in the 1980 *Journal of Youth and Adolescence*, showed that small schools (of approximately 500 students) also have lower incidence of crime and less serious student misconduct. Larger schools (with 1,000 or more students), on the other hand, discourage a sense of responsibility and meaningful participation, particularly among students who have academic difficulty and come from lower socioeconomic backgrounds.

William Fowler (1992) stated that the effects of school size at the elementary school level seem conclusive based upon "the general

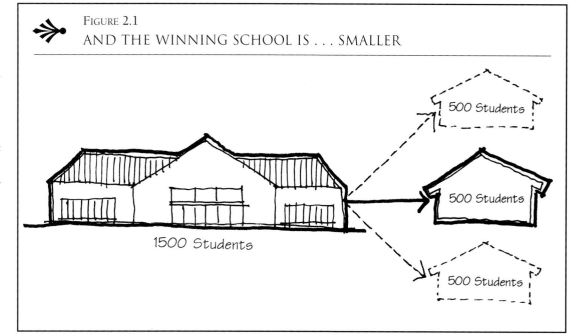

FIGURE 2.1
AND THE WINNING SCHOOL IS . . . SMALLER

1500 Students

500 Students

500 Students

500 Students

THE PUBLIC EDUCATION ASSOCIATION AND OTHERS RECOMMEND DOWNSIZING ELEMENTARY AND MIDDLE SCHOOLS TO 500 TO 600 STUDENTS PER SCHOOL, ARGUING THAT SMALLER SCHOOLS LEAD TO A MORE HUMANE EDUCATIONAL SYSTEM.

agreement of the findings." Fowler summarized the literature by reporting that (1) there is a negative relationship between math and verbal test scores and elementary school size, (2) larger elementary schools are detrimental to student achievement, (3) smaller elemen-

14

tary schools are particularly beneficial to African American students' achievement, and (4) the negative relationship between school size and school performance is most prevalent in urban schools.

Paul Goldberger's (1990) review of the design competition in *New Schools for New York* concluded, "Educators have begun to suggest that the real sin in contemporary school design is size—the winning school is . . . smaller."

THE SCHOOL AS A COMMUNITY HUB / NECKLACE OF COMMUNITY ACTIVITIES

Although we found no empirical research on the topic, a number of reform commentators have suggested that one of the important new educational directions for the 21st century is making the school a community hub.

Ted Fiske, in *Smart Schools, Smart Kids* (1991), describes a number of innovative "learning communities" turning schools into centers for child advocacy, including some 70 community organizations dealing with health, social services, recreation, and housing.

Several new schools and many on the drawing boards for New York City reflect this idea. The *American School Board Journal* (Berg and Apostle 1991) reported that the construction of community recreation centers as part of schools is a solution for building community support for public education among a growing number

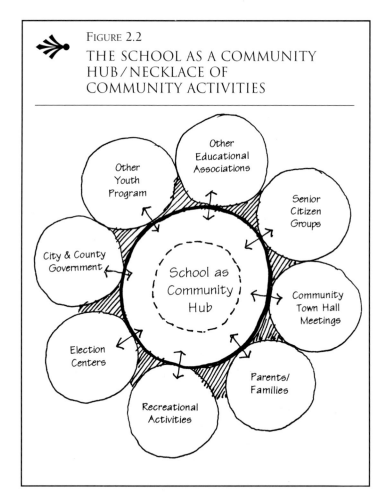

FIGURE 2.2

THE SCHOOL AS A COMMUNITY HUB / NECKLACE OF COMMUNITY ACTIVITIES

THE SCHOOL IS RAPIDLY BECOMING A HUB FOR COMMUNITY ACTIVITIES—A LEARNING COMMUNITY FOR CHILD AND ADULT DAY CARE, HEALTH AND OTHER SOCIAL SERVICES, YOUTH PROGRAMS, TOWN HALL MEETINGS, RECREATION, AND EVEN HOUSING. ARCHITECTURALLY, THE SCHOOL MAY WRAP AROUND THE COMMUNITY FUNCTIONS AS AROUND A "TOWN SQUARE"; OR THE COMMUNITY FUNCTIONS MAY BECOME A "NECKLACE" AROUND THE SCHOOL.

of community residents who do not have children in school. Centers are scheduled so everyone in the community can use them, including adult education programs and senior citizen groups. New schools include child care centers, continuing and job training programs, youth programs, programs for parents and families, administration offices, social services, and facilities for community and town hall meetings. In essence, the old "school" becomes a "community hub," a community education and service center.

Architecturally, the school may wrap around the community functions, as around a "town square"; or the community functions may be a "necklace" around the school. At the Lago Lindo School in Edmonton, a simple urban piazza connects the school to a future community building, creating a focal point for the community. This community relationship encourages the use of the school year-round, both for primary education and community functions, in response to a wish for a broadening and deepening sense of community—with the school as a lifelong learning community.

TEAM SUITES/CLUSTERS OF CLASSROOMS

The classroom suite, sometimes called the "Self-Contained Classroom Community" or "The Pod School," is another common reform idea. The philosophy behind this reform idea and corresponding design prototype is that teachers and students together constitute a small community. The architectural manifestation is a series of small suites of classrooms and support facilities around the central core functions of the school. Support facilities might include lounges, informal learning spaces, a computer hub, office space for teachers, lockers, bathrooms, display cases, and seminar rooms. Layouts can accommodate different teams and community philosophies: classrooms can vary with relation to size and openness, the relationship of the teachers' offices to classroom space, and so on.

Strickland & Carson Associates' design for School Site Number 1 in the Bronx, reported in *New Schools for New York* (Genevro 1992), includes suites for an inner-city school, each with classrooms, lounge space, office space for teachers, lockers, private bathrooms, window seats, terraces, hallway display cases, and small seminar rooms. This design prototype, and this pattern, reflect the idea that teachers and students constitute a small community or a "family" in a "house."

SUPERVISABLE CIRCULATION PATHS

Confusing circulation patterns impede children's use of schools and create unnecessary chaos and disorganization. The central educational issue regarding circulation is maximization of time on task, particularly during lesson transitions. Paul Gump (1987) found that students were off task more in open-plan schools (i.e., schools with-

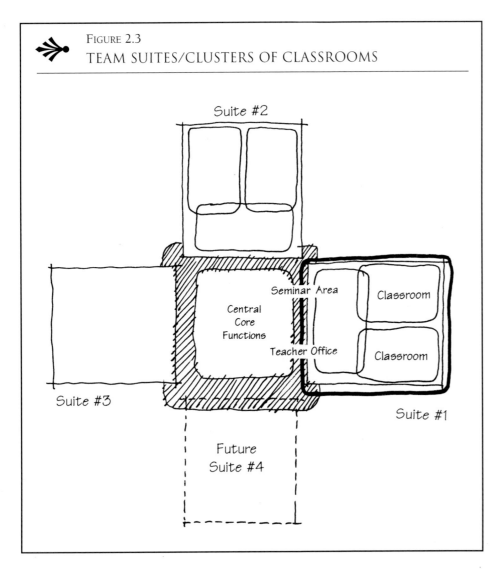

FIGURE 2.3
TEAM SUITES/CLUSTERS OF CLASSROOMS

Suite #2

Seminar Area   Classroom

Central
Core
Functions

Teacher Office   Classroom

Suite #3

Suite #1

Future
Suite #4

out walls) than in closed-plan schools (those with self-contained classrooms),
with much time lost in transition between activities. Various design researchers suggest that circulation patterns surrounding activities encourage children to look around and see what is available, and that fluid traffic patterns provide a means for better communication. It is anticipated that more teacher-to-teacher communication and a wider variety of interaction among students and between students and learning materials will occur in schools with clear, well-planned circulation paths.

Supervisability, however, is a major problem for teachers and administrators in many schools. Educators want circulation corridors that provide opportunities for learning through activity pockets for free-standing display cases, wall-mounted tack-boards, and pockets off the main corridor with vision glass into specialty classrooms. In certain settings, however, the desire for circulation that serves educational or functional needs must be bal-

A SERIES OF SMALL SUITES OF INTERCONNECTING, INTER-
COMMUNICATING CLASSROOMS AND SUPPORT FACILITIES
CENTER AROUND CORE FUNCTIONS IN WHICH TEACHERS
AND STUDENTS TOGETHER CONSTITUTE A SMALL COMMUNITY.

anced with the need for supervision and the reality of frequent vandalism For example, when architects design corridors and recessed doorways to minimize hallway length, students can hide in various nooks and crannies located off the corridors out of the sight of teachers or safety supervisors. When possible, therefore, the circulation path should be cleared of visually obstructing objects to facilitate effective supervision.

 ## SMALL CLASSROOMS

Any review of the considerable research on classroom size leads to an unmistakable conclusion—smaller is better. William Fowler (1992), of the Department of Education's Office of Educational Research and Improvement, summarized the literature on class size and concluded that students' attitudes, achievement, and voluntary participation increase in small classrooms (of 20 or fewer students). In small classrooms, teachers have more interactions with each student; can provide a rich and vastly differing array of interactions; and can implement learning centers, student learning teams, peer tutorials, and other instructional strategies. On the other hand, higher absolute density and greater perceived crowding have been associated with

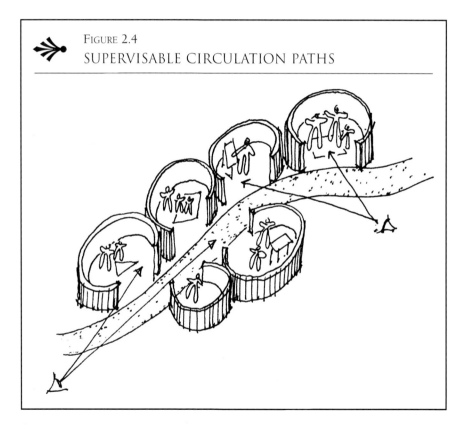

FIGURE 2.4
SUPERVISABLE CIRCULATION PATHS

SUPERVISABLE CIRCULATION PATHS BALANCE THE NEED FOR CLEAR CIRCULATION BETWEEN ALL ACTIVITIES IN THE SCHOOL AND THE NEED FOR SUPERVISION TO DECREASE UNDESIRABLE AND DANGEROUS BEHAVIORS.

decreased attention, lower task performance, behavioral problems, and social withdrawal. As Carol Weinstein (1979, p. 585) noted, "Nowhere else are large groups of individuals packed so closely together for so many hours, yet expected to perform at peak efficiency on different learning tasks and to interact harmoniously."

Project STAR, a four-year study that followed 6,500 students in Tennessee from kindergarten through 3rd grade (Finn and Achilles 1990), found that children in smaller classes (13 to 17 per room) outperformed those in regular-sized classes (22 to 25 per room) as measured by achievement test scores. In the early grades, children in smaller classes performed better in all subjects, particularly in reading and mathematics, with smaller classes especially

FIGURE 2.5
SMALL CLASSROOMS

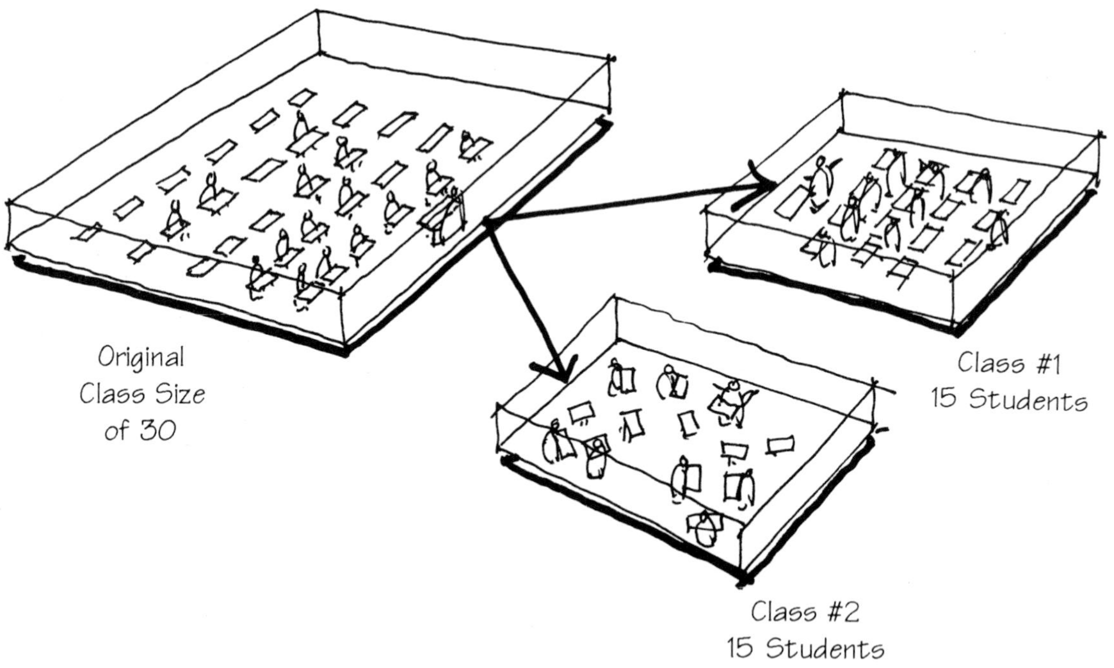

Original Class Size of 30

Class #1
15 Students

Class #2
15 Students

RESEARCH INDICATES THAT SMALLER CLASSROOMS (FEWER THAN 20 STUDENTS, ESPECIALLY THOSE WITH 13 TO 17 STUDENTS) LEAD TO IMPROVED STUDENT ATTITUDES, HIGHER ACHIEVEMENT SCORES, AND GREATER TEACHER SATISFACTION AND MORALE, AND AFFORD DIFFERENT AND VARIED INSTRUCTIONAL PRACTICES.

helpful for children in inner-city schools. And while the improvement was immediately clear in small kindergarten rooms, the benefits increased in 1st grade and remained stable through 3rd grade.

Glass and associates (1982) conducted a meta-analysis of a
collection of studies on class size, which indicated that reducing
class size from 30 to 20 students can yield a gain of 6 percentage
points on achievement scores, whereas a reduction from 20 to 10
students per classroom yields an additional 13 percentage points.
The analysts concluded that the greatest differences in learning
achievement are achieved by limiting class size to no more than 15
students.

PORTFOLIO PROCESS STUDIOS

As schools move beyond traditional assessment strategies and standardized achievement tests, alternative assessment models such as
portfolios (advocated by such reformers as Grant Wiggins and Holly
Houston of the Center on Learning, Assessment, and School
Structure; Ted Sizer of the Coalition of Essential Schools; and many
others) are becoming commonplace. Portfolios are considered a
more authentic means of testing the process as well as the final
product of student work. Advocates believe they are more aligned
with real-world situations and enable students to effectively show
what they have actually learned.

The design implications for portfolios and other alternative

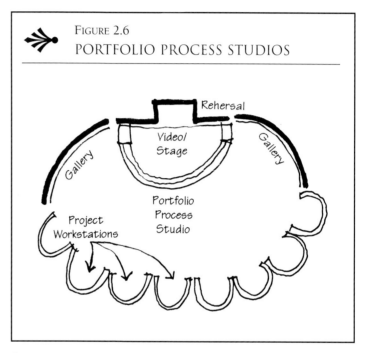

FIGURE 2.6
PORTFOLIO PROCESS STUDIOS

THE DEMANDS FOR AUTHENTIC TESTING REQUIRE APPROPRIATE SPACE FOR
WORKING ON AND EXHIBITING PORTFOLIOS, INCLUDING A/V STUDIOS,
PERFORMANCE STUDIOS, INDIVIDUAL PROJECT WORK SPACE, LARGE OPEN
PROJECT TABLES, A GALLERY TO DISPLAY WORK, AND A STAGING AREA

forms of assessment include the need to provide appropriate space
for working on, storing, and exhibiting student work. This space
must accommodate a wide range of activities and products, including, but not limited to, audio/visual studio productions, live performances, mathematics projects, individual project work, large open
project tables, a gallery to display work, and staging areas.

TO SUPPORT SHARED DECISION MAKING,
PROFESSIONALISM AMONG TEACHERS,
AND A LEARNING COMMUNITY, PRIVATE
TEACHER OFFICES MAY BE CLUSTERED
AND SHARE A COMMON SEMINAR SPACE,
MEETING ROOM, AND STAFF BACKSTAGE.

CLUSTERS OF TEACHER OFFICES

Education reformers increasingly
recognize the need for a new professionalism among teachers. In
The Condition of Teaching, the
Carnegie Foundation for the
Advancement of Teaching (1988b)
found that the nation's teachers
"see themselves less involved in
key school decisions, find work-
ing conditions unsatisfactory, and give the reform movement itself
low marks." Ernest Boyer, president of the foundation, concluded:
"Improved working conditions are essential if we hope to attract and
hold outstanding teachers. They must be regarded as professionals,
treated as professionals, and consider themselves to be professionals.
Unless we create an environment in the schools . . . that sustains

such an attitude, we cannot expect improvements to occur."

If teachers are to be involved not only in direct classroom
teaching, but also in selecting textbooks and other aspects of shared
decision making and professional development, they must have
quality, private working space (including telephones, fax machines,
computer terminals, etc.).

FIGURE 2.7
CLUSTERS OF TEACHER OFFICES

Common Office Space

Classroom · Office · Conf. · Office · Classroom · Office · Office · Classroom · Classroom

--OR--

Classroom · Office · Conf. · Office · Classroom · Office · Office · Classroom · Classroom

FIGURE 2.8
ORIGIN AND STATUS OF 27 DESIGN PATTERNS

	Justification: Architectural Literature	Educational Reform Literature	E/B Research	Practical Experience	Status: Confidence Rating
Planning Issues					
And the Winning School is...Smaller	None	Strong	Strong	Strong	***
School as a Community Center/ Necklace of Community Activities	Some	Strong	None	None	**
Contextual Compatability	Some	None	None	None	*
Safe Location	None	None	Some	None	**
Building Organizing Principles					
Campus-Plan Concept/ Schools Within Schools	Some	Some	Some	None	**
Compact Building Form	Strong	None	None	None	*
Building Core/Community Forum	Some	Some	None	None	*
Team Suites/Clusters of Classrooms	Some	Strong	None	None	***
Great Spaces	Strong	None	None	None	*
Modified Open Space	None	None	Some	Some	**
Supervisable Circulation Paths	Strong	None	None	Strong	**
Flexible/Adaptable Learning Facility	Strong	Strong	None	Strong	**
Home as a Template for School	Some	None	None	None	*
Design Diversity	Some	None	None	None	*
Character of Individual Spaces					
Small Classrooms	None	Strong	Strong	Strong	***
Variety of Learning Centers	None	Some	None	Some	**
Well-Defined Activity Areas	None	None	Some	None	**
Table Groups	None	None	Some	Some	**
Nested Classroom Groupings	None	Some	None	None	**
Portfolio Process Studios	None	Strong	None	None	**
Administration in the Mainstream	None	Some	None	None	*
Cluster of Teacher Offices	None	Strong	None	Some	**
Indoor-Outdoor Transition Spaces	Some	None	None	None	**
User-Friendly/Child-Centered Aesthetics and Scale	Some	None	None	None	**
Critical Technical Details					
Indoor Climate	Strong	None	Some	Some	***
Appropriate Acoustics	Strong	None	Some	Strong	***
Natural/Full-Spectrum Lighting	Strong	None	Some	Some	**

KEY

Magnitude of Justification
- ● Strong
- ◑ Some
- ○ None
- ▢ Patterns discussed in chapter

Confidence Rating
- *** Very Confident
- ** Moderately Confident
- * Slightly Confident

PATTERNS FOR REFORM

These seven design patterns have potential for use in the design of new school facilities and the renovation or expansion of existing schools. Figure 2.8 presents the origins and status of the 27 patterns we generated prior to the publication of this chapter, with highlights for the 7 presented here. We have identified appropriate references for the origin of each pattern and consider each a working hypothesis, subject to testing and refutation or corroboration. Figure 2.8 reports overall confidence ratings in the validity of each pattern based on the strength of its current support in the educational reform and environment-behavior literatures for use by educators and architectural professionals.

The development and use of design patterns should be seen as a collaborative dialogue between researchers and practitioners from the architectural and educational professions. The design patterns presented here represent a fraction of the number of patterns that we and our students have subsequently developed. Additional patterns have likely resulted from the work of other architects and educational researchers over the last 10 years of educational reform but have not yet been articulated. Further, new design patterns will continue to emerge from the feedback of students, teachers, and administrators in school facilities as they struggle to implement reform ideas. Including students and teachers in the process of identifying and creating design patterns will further increase the number of reform-based design patterns. Educators and policymakers can benefit from such awareness, as the success of the educational reforms of the 1990s will depend, in part, on the support these reform programs receive from the physical settings in which they are placed.

References

Barker, R., and P.V. Gump. (1964). *Big School, Small School.* Palo Alto, Calif.: Stanford University Press.

Berg, H.M., and T. Apostle. (November 1991). "Third Time Lucky: How a Savvy Bond Issue Campaign Helped Us Build New Schools." *American School Board Journal* 178, 11: 54–56.

California Department of Education. (1990). *Schools for the 21st Century.* Sacramento: Author, Bureau of Publications.

Carnegie Foundation for the Advancement of Teaching. (1988a). *An Imperiled Generation: Saving Urban Schools.* Princeton, N.J.: Author.

Carnegie Foundation for the Advancement of Teaching. (1988b). *The Condition of Teaching: A State-by-State Analysis.* Princeton, N.J.: Author.

District of Columbia Commission on Public Education. (1989). *Our Children, Our Future: Revitalizing the District of Columbia Public Schools.* Washington, D.C.: Author.

Finn, J.D., and C.M. Achilles. (1990). "Answers and Questions About Class Size: A Statewide Experiment." *American Educational Research Journal* 27: 557–577.

Fiske, E.B. (1991). *Smart Schools, Smart Kids: Why Do Some Schools Work?* New York: Simon & Schuster.

Fowler Jr., W.J. (1992). "What Do We Know About School Size? What Should We Know?" Washington, D.C.: Office of Educational Research and Improvement, National Center for Educational Statistics, U.S. Department of Education.

Garbarino, J. (1980). "Some Thoughts on School Size and Its Effects on Adolescent Development." *Journal of Youth and Adolescence* 9: 19–31.

Genevro, R. (1990). "New York City School Designs: A Project of the Architectural League of New York and the Public Education Association—New Schools for New York." *Teachers College Record* 92: 248–271.

Genevro, R., ed. (1992). *New Schools for New York: Plans and Precedents for Small Schools.* New York: Princeton Architectural Press.

Glass, G.V., L.S. Cahen, M.L. Smith, and N.N. Filby. (1982). *School Class Size: Research and Policy.* Beverly Hills, Calif.: Sage.

Goldberger, P. (May 27, 1990). "Review of the Design Competition on New Schools for New York." *New York Times,* Part II, 23: 1.

Gump, P.V. (1987). "School and Classroom Environments." In *Handbook of Environmental Psychology,* edited by D. Stokols and I. Altman. New York: Wiley.

Moore, G.T., and J.A. Lackney. (1993). "Blueprints for School Success: How Size and Location of Schools Affect Achievement." *Rethinking Schools* 7, 4: 21.

Moore, G.T., and J.A. Lackney. (1993). "School Design: Crisis, Educational Performance, and Design Patterns." *Children's Environments* 10, 2: 99–112

Moore, G.T. (Summer 1995). In the periodical *Edutopia,* published by the George Lucas Educational Foundation.

Weinstein, C.S. (1979). "The Physical Environment of the School: A Review of the Research." *Review of Educational Research* 49: 577–10.

PLACE AS A FORM OF KNOWLEDGE

STEVEN BINGLER

ARCHITECTURE IS A REPOSITORY FOR MATHEMATICAL EQUATIONS, SCIENTIFIC PRINCIPLES, HISTORICAL REFERENCES, GEOGRAPHICAL DESIGN DETERMINANTS, AND LITERARY CONTENT. IT IS ALSO A LOT OF FUN.

One of the most pressing questions concerning the programming and design of educational facilities centers around whether facilities play any significant role in the learning process. The conventional wisdom of superintendents and school boards is that educational facilities simply provide the containers in which learning occurs, but that the form of the containers, and even the process of making them, has little to contribute to the real purpose of education, which centers around the curriculum and instruction delivered by the educator and received by the student. Recent thinking about learning, however, places more emphasis on the student as the center of the learning process and on heuristic curriculums that involve all sorts of objects and projects integral to the discovery process. Therefore, it may be time to look again at buildings as learning tools. After all, over $10 billion is spent annually on the design and construction of educational facilities. This seems like a lot of money to waste on containers. The challenge then is one of design and creativity. In the best of all worlds, the facilities that we build to house the educational process would also serve as a form of knowledge and as an instrument of curriculum and instruction in the learning process.

This design and creativity can be accomplished in almost limitless ways because architecture embodies such a multitude of disciplines. During the Renaissance, architecture was referred to as "frozen music," and it has often been called the "mother of the arts." Architecture is a repository for mathematical equations, scientific principles, historical references, geographical design determinants, and literary content. It is also a lot of fun. The designing and building process has often been used as a motivating force for individuals and even groups of individuals. Consider, for example, the process of "barn raising," which has served as a social event for communal

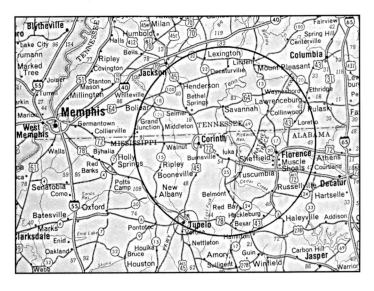

empowerment. All of these concepts and more are available for the asking, and can help all of the facilities that we build contribute significantly to a broad spectrum of learning needs.

Perhaps a working example is the best way to illustrate this idea. The small town of Iuka, in northeastern Mississippi, is the seat of government for Tishomingo County, which has a population of 20,000 people whose average annual income is less than $13,000 per family. Tishomingo County is itself a form of knowledge. Its rich cultural heritage is filled with Native American, Appalachian, and southern folkways. Its traditions are close to the earth.

For thousands of years, Tishomingo County was the homeland of the Chickasaw nation. The Chickasaws had settled there to be near a group of mineral springs believed to have special medicinal powers. Chiefs Iuka and Tishomingo played an important role in leading the tribe through a difficult struggle with the incoming white settlers that ended with a complete relocation of the Chickasaw civilization to Oklahoma in the early part of the 19th century.

Railroad entrepreneurs quickly recognized the value of the healing springs and located a health spa there that led to the development of the town of Iuka. The railroad played an important role in the development of the region's natural resources for more than 100 years.

MAP SHOWING LOCATION OF IUKA, MISSISSIPPI, WHERE COLLABORATIVE PLANNING YIELDED A MULTIPURPOSE COMMUNITY EDUCATION CENTER.

THE MINERAL SPRINGS WERE IMPORTANT TO THE NATIVE AMERICAN CULTURE AND TO THE RAILROAD ENTREPRENEURS WHO BUILT A HEALTH SPA IN IUKA.

funds used for constructing educational facilities. My involvement began when the Department of Economic and Community Development, charged with administering the funds, called on my firm, Concordia Architects, to work with local architects on the facility's design.

 ## BEGINNING THE DESIGN PROCESS

The design process began in Tishomingo County with a series of brainstorming sessions that Concordia architects held with students, parents, teachers, and representatives from the community at large. We drank a lot of punch and listened as folks told us about Chiefs Iuka and Tishomingo. They were clearly curious about the region's history, and proud of it. The sports teams are called the "Braves," even though no Native Americans still live in the region, and many people collect Native American artifacts such as arrowheads and old pottery shards.

In 1989, a third chapter in the region's growth was inaugurated by NASA's decision to locate its new $1.4 billion solid rocket motor facility in Tishomingo County just 20 miles north of Iuka. Also in 1989, through a special Economic Impact Authority, the Mississippi State legislature allocated over $25 million to improve community infrastructure in the northeast region, with most of the

THE SCHOOL
CAME TO
RESEMBLE A
COMMUNITY
CENTER, WITH
A 120-FOOT
DIAMETER
CIRCULAR
PLAZA
SERVING AS
THE NEXUS
OF THE
COMMUNITY
LEARNING
CENTER
COMPLEX.

When we asked what the community needed the most from a new educational facility, we got a broad range of responses. Students said they would like their learning environment to be more fun. They were tired of feeling as if they were in prison all day. Parents wanted more things for their kids to do in the mornings and evenings. They complained that the children in Tishomingo County didn't have enough options when it came to entertainment and that the older kids were spending too much time driving to find things to do. The parents also wished something could be done to engage students more and motivate them to learn. Perhaps their greatest dream was for an educational system that could prepare their children for meaningful careers closer to home.

Teachers wanted flexibility. One group of citizens felt that the community really needed a theater. Another group had been meeting for months trying to raise funds to build a YMCA. A third contingent noted that the only place to hold a party or wedding reception for more than 50 people was the roller skating rink. And the list went

on. By the time the programming process was finished, a contingent of about 30 people from the brainstorming groups had organized themselves as the Community Action Team (CAT) and began legal proceedings to seek 501(c)(3) nonprofit status.

EARLY PLANNING LED TO THE FORMATION OF A COMMUNITY ACTION TEAM, SHOWN HERE REVIEWING SITE PLANS.

✦ CREATING INITIAL PLANS

It was time to begin laying out some plans. The School Board had purchased a 100-acre parcel of land a few miles west of Iuka as the site for the new high school. Here, Concordia Architects led the design process, working with the local firm of Johnson, Bailey Architects. As the sketches evolved, the school came to resemble a community center, with a 120-foot diameter circular plaza serving as the nexus of the community learning center complex. On the northwest side of the plaza is a freestanding 450-seat auditorium that doubles as a community theater. Through a generous grant from Paul

Newman and Joanne Woodward and the labor of local volunteers, the theater was outfitted to support professional productions. On the northeast side is a gymnasium that also serves as the community fitness center. The cafeteria, which also fronts on the plaza, is designed with a "hunting lodge" decor, complete with a large triangular fireplace built of native "Tishomingo" stone, and it functions as a

ARCHITECTURAL MODEL OF THE TISHOMINGO COUNTY EDUCATION COMPLEX.

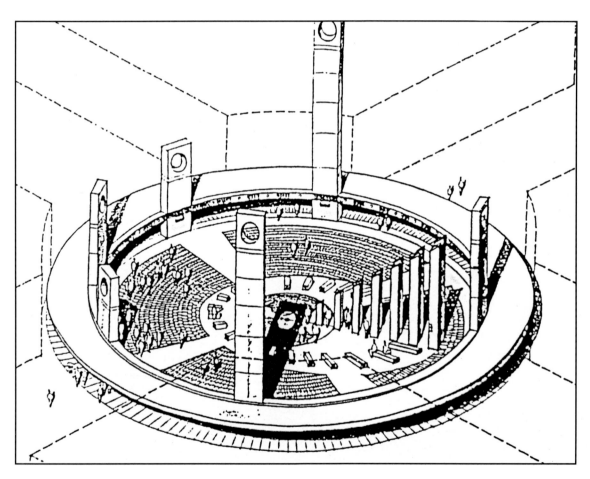

community entertainment and conference center. On the southeast quadrant of the plaza lies the media center and classroom building where movable partitions allow teachers to join up to four classrooms together for team teaching and cooperative learning.

To the southwest is a special adult education center operated by the University of Mississippi, which brings college courses to the Tishomingo community. The University Center is also occupied by the Tri-State Learning Center (TLC, for short), which serves as a teacher and student resource center for NASA's recently inaugurated 9,000-square-mile

LIKE ITS EDUCATIONAL HARDWARE, TISHOMINGO COUNTY'S NEW CURRICULUM WILL ADDRESS A BROAD RANGE OF COMMUNITY NEEDS.

Tri-State Education Initiative. To the south of the University Center lies a freestanding Child Development Center with a community-based curriculum focused on intelligence, motor skills, and personality development. High school students are encouraged to sign up for special credits in vocational child care and parenting skills.

The exterior of all of the buildings in the complex was designed using a combination of brick and native "Tishomingo" stone. Eight-inch square openings at two-foot intervals accommodate a series of hand-print castings organized by the Community Action Team. The hand-print committee persuaded the vo-tech students to build the wooden molds for the castings and organized the local Ladies' Club and Lions Club to entice local citizens to make their permanent marks on the new facility. At $20 per casting, the committee has made over 450 castings and donated the $9,000 in proceeds to the media center.

A covered walkway links the four independent structures around the perimeter of the circular plaza. In honor of the great environmental heritage of the Chickasaw nation, the interior of the plaza has been designed as a giant sundial and solar observatory. When additional funding has been raised and the solar observatory is completed, the plaza will serve as an integrated learning labora-tory for the study of mathematics, science, history, and social studies. Here, students of all ages will study the geometry of the universe in motion, geographical and astronomical alignments, celestial navigation, Native American history, and social studies in an immediate and multidisciplinary way.

A 50-acre environmental learning park at the eastern entrance to the circular plaza is being built by a team of local residents, teachers, and students. When complete, the park will include outdoor classrooms, a wildlife feeding and rehabilitation station, extensive nature trails, beehives, birdhouses, a replica of a Chickasaw Indian village, and a performing arts amphitheater.

The school district plans to raise funds to develop a full-scale cultural and environmental curriculum and a "user's manual" for the many learning tools soon to be at its disposal. Like its educational hardware, Tishomingo County's new curriculum will address a broad range of community needs. To the degree possible, it will address the future development of the Tishomingo County region by providing job training that will allow citizens to pursue their interests and careers on their home turf.

In the meantime, the Tishomingo County Education Complex is like a barn raising work-in-progress. Students, parents, teachers, and local business people are continuing to work for their community. Besides the ongoing environmental learning park and cultural museum projects, volunteers have landscaped the entire grounds of the new facility and built a football and baseball field. A separate committee received a grant from the state to create a local

Tishomingo County Arts Council. Its first year's cultural season opened with a live production of the ballet *The Nutcracker* in the new community theater. Other performances have included the Oxford Piano Trio and Neil Simon's *The Good Doctor*. Season tickets to all performances sold out and two productions were planned especially for students.

"It's the first time most of our students have ever seen a live professional performance" says Bob Haggard, principal of the new learning center. "It's hard to say exactly what's happening, but the students are definitely interested in what's going on here. Even though the solar observatory isn't built yet, we have had groups of teachers and students coming back here at night to study the stars. This year 40 out of the 70 science awards in the state science fair went to Tishomingo County students."

Bob Ferguson, superintendent of Tishomingo County schools put it another way: "There is a lot of pride in this facility on the part of everyone in the community. I believe it's because they know that it was planned especially for them. Even the students treat the place with respect. There are no graffiti, no skid marks, and negligible vandalism. Beyond that, the facility seems to promote academics somehow. I don't know whether it's because there are so many adults around that maybe it feels more like a part of everyday life. Maybe it has something to do with the design of the buildings. The kids still love their sports activities, but there is something different going on. But don't ask me to explain it; that would be like asking me how a radio works."

. . . IT IS BECAUSE
OUR MEMORIES
OF FORMER
DWELLING-PLACES
ARE RELIVED AS
DAYDREAMS
THAT THESE
DWELLING-PLACES
OF THE PAST
REMAIN IN US
FOR ALL TIME.

—GASTON BACHELARD
IN *THE POETICS OF SPACE*

(1969)

USING CULTURAL INFORMATION TO CREATE SCHOOLS THAT WORK

4

SARA SNYDER CRUMPACKER

The feelings we once experienced in a place can be called to mind by something as simple as a smell, a picture, a song, or a sound. Such fleeting reminders evoke strong images of places from our pasts. Think of the school of your youth: Was there a favorite tree outside a classroom window you watched drop its leaves and stand bareheaded all winter, only to be born again in spring's glorious bloom? Perhaps you can recall the tantalizing sound of glass milk bottles clanking against wire crates as snacks were being delivered; the mouth-watering aroma of peanut butter cookies baking in cafeteria ovens; or the secret place behind a hall fire extinguisher where you wrote your name? If places have such lasting effects on people's lives, then it makes sense that those places in which we spend time should be designed expressly for us. In schools this means designs that inspire good teaching, support productive learning, enhance people's joy, and prompt feelings of security.

Even though schools are used by students and teachers, few buildings are actually designed with them in mind. Facility planners get caught in hundreds of distracting demands—state mandates, local building codes, site assessments, energy efficiency ratios, and maintenance considerations. The people who will live their lives in a new or renovated facility are forgotten or, at best, have only token representation on a down-the-line, power-diluted planning committee.

THE STUDY OF
SCHOOL AS PLACE

I have studied the cultures of schools to find out what people in each setting need to support their daily living. I watch the behavior patterns and listen to the stories of people as they live and work at school.[1] After all, they are the experts on their own environments. From them, I try to discover answers to questions like these: What is the school all about from the viewpoint of its users? What common assumptions do they have? How do people organize their daily living in the building? In what activities do they engage? What perspectives do they share? How do they describe and explain their world? What are the inventions and creations people use to make their school environments work for them?

Then I give the answers to these questions to architects and planners to allow them to draft case-relevant solutions for their design projects. Actually, I discover the unspoken, commonsense information users carry with them, and then make it explicit and obvious—ready for facility planners to use in their work. This insider information far exceeds the normal head, resource, and program counts used as bottom-line information in most school planning.

[1]Further information on methodologies can be found in "The Experience of School as Place," an unpublished doctoral dissertation by Sara Snyder Crumpacker, University of Virginia, 1992.

 ## PLANNING INFORMATION
DERIVED FROM CULTURAL STUDIES

Cultural research has been used successfully in facility planning for businesses and other organizations for years. For example, in 1979, when Corning Glass decided to build a new engineering facility at its headquarters in New York (see Brenner 1981 and Liebson 1981), company managers hired consultants to study the behavior patterns of engineering and research employees who would be working at the new building. Some of their findings revealed that:

- Impromptu work sessions were often held at water coolers and coffee stations;
- Engineers got over 80 percent of their information from direct, face-to-face contact with their peers (rather than from publications and seminars); and
- Workers didn't travel more than 100 feet from their own desks to confer with others and hated using the telephone to get information.

As a result of these observations and other user information, plans for the new Corning building included several elements to facilitate communication:

- Break stations equipped with writing boards, markers, and erasers. These write-on surfaces and tools encourage employees to jot

down, sketch out, and discuss their ideas during chance encounters.
- A central atrium, making the building visibly open between floors, and clear glass partitions throughout the building, which foster a sense of community and accessibility.
- Strategically located stairways, ramps, and elevator banks to keep distances and times between colleagues short.

Despite the effective use of cultural information in the design of business offices, school planners and architects have become alert to its merits only recently.

I began my research on school cultures in 1990. What I have learned is fascinating. While my discoveries are case-specific, some of the findings suggest ideas that teachers and principals can adapt to their existing classrooms and buildings.

Homes Should Be Templates for Schools

Students and educators prefer homelike features to help them interpret daily living at school. Clothes closets in rooms rather than lockers in halls, ruffled curtains in windows, old-fashioned screen doors, soft places to sit, live plants and flowers, pets, attention to decorating details, food smells from the cafeteria, hooks for aprons, and pictures and trophies hung on walls where they can be touched instead of stored behind glass in locked showcases all felt like home to people in schools. Homelike surroundings can facilitate family-like interactions, too. Assigned chores—cleaning the blackboards,

passing out papers, emptying the trash, washing the cafeteria tables—add a dimension of home and make students feel needed as part of the culture.

By taking a look at the homes of those who will eventually use the school, we can find out what represents homelike surroundings to them: What makes them comfortable? What nourishes their senses and nurtures their souls? It may be something as simple as a potted red geranium's spot of color on an apartment window sill, the feel of an old velvet sofa on a sunlit back porch, or the smell of ethnic food wafting in from a deli around the corner. Homelike features in schools facilitate the successful transition of users from their home environments to their learning environments.

Animals Play a Significant Role in Children's Lives

In urban and rural schools I've found that children have a strong affinity for animals. For kids in the country, animals are such a normal part of life that they want them around all the time—at school as well as home. One school I studied had hamsters rolling out of room doors and down hallways in clear plastic balls. When found out of their territory, the animals were simply returned to their classroom residence. While some animals were officially sanctioned by members of the building culture, other uninvited guests found their ways inside the school in pockets and lunch pails. Many were given permanent lodgings by indulgent and savvy teachers with a requirement of their adoption being that students take responsibility for the care of these creatures.

PARENTS
AND TEACHERS
REPORTED
A LOWER
INCIDENCE OF
FIGHTING AT
HOME AND
SCHOOL,
INCREASED
RESPECT FOR
ADULTS, AND
IMPROVED
GRADES.

Strong needs for animals were expressed by students in urban settings as well. A large number of children attending city schools live in apartments where pets are banned. These boys and girls have no opportunity at home to interact with animals larger than turtles or gerbils. Children in one densely populated Northern Virginia community told me imaginary stories of an "animal room" in their school. They populated their fantasy with creatures previously only read about in books.

Impressive testimony documents the student-animal theme I discovered.

The Animal Companion Project in Dade County, Florida. In 1987, after 26 years as a veterinarian, Dick Dillman volunteered to work with 15 at-risk 6th grade boys in Miami. Identified by teachers and counselors, these students had attendance rates of less than 50 percent, low academic achievement, and poor attitudes about teachers and school. Dillman promised the boys one morning a week working with farm animals for every four days they spent in school. The rules governing the program were simple: respect, trust, sensitivity, and responsi-

bility. The students' work with live animals was coordinated with the study of science, and the program was designed to build the kids' self-esteem, promote good moral values, and improve their academic performance, attendance, attitudes, and behavior.

At the end of the program's first year, the attendance rate for these boys had jumped to over 90 percent! Parents and teachers reported a lower incidence of fighting at home and school, increased respect for adults, and improved grades. The only real problem Dillman encountered was excitement—he had trouble controlling the boys' enthusiasm. At this writing, the Animal Companion program —supported by a grant from the Kellogg Foundation to the Miami-Dade Community College—serves 270 boys and girls, including learning-disabled and emotionally disturbed youngsters, from 18 Dade County elementary schools. The expanded program now includes Saturday visits to nursing homes with domestic animals, a horseback riding academy, and programs for special-needs youngsters.

The Green Chimneys Project in Brewster, New York. Sam Ross runs a residential farm for children who are educationally, emotionally, and physically handicapped or from dysfunctional families. The children interact with and are responsible for over 200 farm animals, wildlife, and domestic pets on this 300-acre spread. Animals act as catalysts in the process of building self-worth, changing behaviors, and re-establishing stability during the two-and-a-half years most children spend on the farm. Green Chimneys has a track record stretching back to 1947.

People Prefer Personal Choices in Environments

In an environment often characterized by denial, delay, and discipline, it's not surprising that people who spend their days in schools often describe and interpret that experience favorably only when they are afforded personal choices. School users prefer areas offering the widest selection of activities, equipment, spaces, supplies, routes, and people possible. Therefore, schools should be planned so that users "bump into" different choices on a daily basis—buildings full of variety, where people experience increased personal satisfaction and comfort because they have some say-so over their daily living. This might mean giving people an opportunity to decide whether to sit in a rocking chair, on an overstuffed sofa, in an old bathtub, or in a loft. It could mean designing alternative routes through the building or different means to the same end: an elevator, a ramp, escalators, and stairs. Facilities offering a variety of choices escape the sterile sameness that characterizes most educational institutions.

Ambient Information Increases Comfort, Understanding, and Learning

Sensory information helps building users interpret their daily living and makes their days predictable—the smell of ditto fluid verifies that the teacher's aide has arrived and gone to work; the sight of the trash truck in the driveway lets everyone know it's Tuesday; and the sound of the band practicing signals to 3rd graders

SCHOOLS SHOULD BE PLANNED SO THAT USERS "BUMP INTO" DIFFERENT CHOICES ON A DAILY BASIS.

that math class is about to begin in their room. The redundancy of this information serves to connect people through their shared knowledge; facilitates feelings of safety, security, and stability at school by letting people know what's going on; and enhances feelings of belonging and ownership.

The sights, sounds, smells, and touches available in a building make it alive for the present and ensure that it will live on as recalled memories later. Who among us does not have a favorite sensory remembrance, which, when experienced in adulthood, propels us back to our days in school? It's also interesting to note that the effectiveness of ambient odors can be used as memory retrieval clues in learning situations (Schab 1990). Rather than compartmentalizing ambient information in airtight, insulated, dead-end spaces, we can heighten awareness by planning for shared sensory experiences in schools.

Smallness Is a Tie That Binds

School users' interpretations are sometimes grounded in smallness. A measure of quantity—physical size and low numbers of people—is what we usually think of as "small." But quantity is only one way of experiencing small. Small also means relationships—feeling like family, being close, sharing connectedness, and trusting. Relationships represent a group of people who come

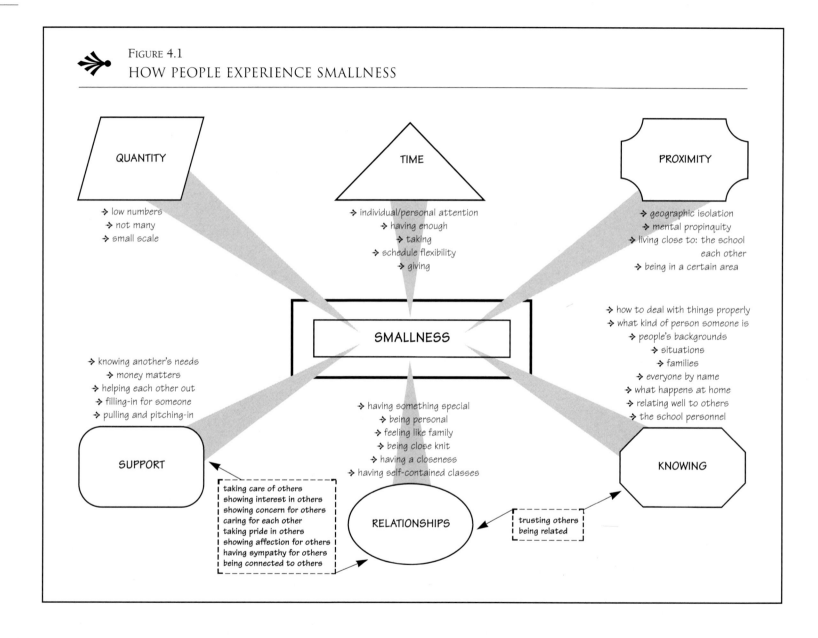

FIGURE 4.1
HOW PEOPLE EXPERIENCE SMALLNESS

QUANTITY

→ low numbers
→ not many
→ small scale

TIME

→ individual/personal attention
→ having enough
→ taking
→ schedule flexibility
→ giving

PROXIMITY

→ geographic isolation
→ mental propinquity
→ living close to: the school
     each other
→ being in a certain area

SMALLNESS

→ how to deal with things properly
→ what kind of person someone is
→ people's backgrounds
→ situations
→ families
→ everyone by name
→ what happens at home
→ relating well to others
→ the school personnel

→ knowing another's needs
→ money matters
→ helping each other out
→ filling-in for someone
→ pulling and pitching-in

→ having something special
→ being personal
→ feeling like family
→ being close knit
→ having a closeness
→ having self-contained classes

SUPPORT

KNOWING

taking care of others
showing interest in others
showing concern for others
caring for each other
taking pride in others
showing affection for others
having sympathy for others
being connected to others

RELATIONSHIPS

trusting others
being related

together, know each other by name, and value each other as individuals. Smallness can mean knowing or having information about others, their backgrounds, and their families. School staffs often believe that knowing or having information about others is synonymous with understanding them.

Smallness is frequently characterized by support. In one school, daily users explained support as showing interest in, caring about, taking care of, showing concern for, helping, taking pride in, showing affection for, and having sympathy for others. Smallness also relates to time: having time to do a good job; taking additional time with a learner; having enough time to be flexible with schedules, spaces, and people; and taking time to give individual or personal attention to others. And smallness involves proximity—both geographical, as in being near each other, and mental, as in being of a like mind or sharing similar perceptions. Both kinds of proximity appear to bind people in a culture closer together.

These discoveries about how people actually experience small can help school planners design buildings that foster feelings of smallness even though the physical size of the building and the number of people using it must be large. Better yet, user revelations about the experience of smallness can point the way for smaller buildings and lower numbers of people in each school.

Schools Should Be Easy to Navigate

Buildings easy to read are easy to use. With no signs to point the way, even first-time visitors want simple ways to navigate

DESIGN CLUES— LIGHTING EFFECTS, VISUAL PERSPECTIVES, DIMENSIONAL DIFFERENCES, FOCAL POINTS— SHOULD SERVE TO DRAW PEOPLE INTO AND THROUGH A BUILDING WITH EASE.

through a building. When we are in personal control of our environment, we're less likely to be disturbed by otherwise stressful elements. We are also more likely to be content and may even be more productive in our endeavors.

Children in one school knew the building so well that they could give visitors directions to all building locations, including infrequently used storage areas for paint, modeling clay, and outdated textbooks. (They knew it so well, in fact, that they even knew how to lower the water pressure in the building.) Design clues—lighting effects, visual perspectives, dimensional differences, focal points—should serve to draw people into and through a building with ease.

Accessibility is equally important to building users. Quick, easy access to people, places, and supplies is essential to getting any job done and to meeting everyone's needs. Such access might mean permanently open doors in public or frequently used spaces, open storage areas for audiovisual and PE equipment, storage places that allow for touching and seeing things throughout the day

FEELINGS OF SAFETY EMANATED FROM THE BUILDING'S OPENNESS RATHER THAN FROM PROTECTIVE FEATURES.

as well as for easy retrieval of items, and materials stored on open shelving rather than hidden away in file drawers or behind cabinet doors.

Privacy Needs Vary by Setting and Person

Needs for privacy vary from school to school and appear to reflect the community in which the school is located. For instance, in urban, densely populated areas, people—particularly students—prefer an occasional place to get away from it all in school. In more rural areas where inhabitants are scattered, school users are less inclined to seek privacy. Rural people often view school as a place to congregate, to share news, and to affirm their membership in the local society.

These differences illustrate the importance of studying specific user cultures prior to each building project rather than jumping to grand, across-the-board generalizations in school planning.

Users Want Unifying Communication Techniques

Most of us prefer the bonding and understanding that results from face-to-face communication. When that isn't possible, school planners need to provide unobtrusive means for communicating

within a building. For example, electronic-mail systems or electronic bulletin boards that can be controlled at the receiving end free teachers and students to focus on their work by making outside communications a service rather than a preemptive mandate.

Almost every school I've been in reflects the need people have to communicate their participation in that school's culture by leaving a mark on the building. These marks are usually individual improvisations such as scribbled messages or autographs in specially chosen places—bathrooms in particular. Designers can include inventive, acceptable ways for people to leave their marks. Projected user-drawn images that can be removed by a flick of a switch or white boards and marking pens placed in strategic locations encourage people to share their personal stories and graffiti in constructive rather than destructive ways. Understanding this user need casts it as a planning opportunity rather than as an administrative problem.

Schools Can Promote Safety and Security Without Enclosing Occupants

In one small school, I made a salient but counterintuitive discovery that feelings of safety emanated from the building's openness rather than from protective features like closed, locked, gated, fenced, or barred enclosures. Daily users were the building's security system—people became the eyes and ears of the school. Because all who belonged were recognized, strangers were easily identified. Any interruption of normal daily activities—a stranger in the building, an unusual sound, a bizarre smell—was cause for concern and someone always checked it out immediately.

The school had long, uninterrupted lines of vision, lots of clear glass windows in and around the building, plenty of ambient sensory information, and a large central room (see Figure 4.2) accessible to everyone. There were no long stretches of hallways, no hidden alcoves, and no unoccupied rooms where a stranger might hide. In this school, people could see and be seen. Everyone was known by name, so relationships were family-like and close rather than institutional and distant. This led to homelike interactions in the building and contributed to feelings of safety.

This plan and versions of it have been used in other settings. Following a careful study of what would facilitate communications and increase personal interaction among building users, University of Wisconsin Organizational Theorist

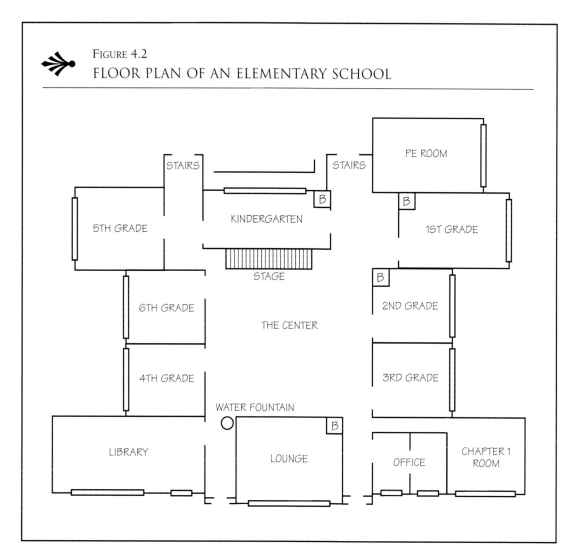

FIGURE 4.2
FLOOR PLAN OF AN ELEMENTARY SCHOOL

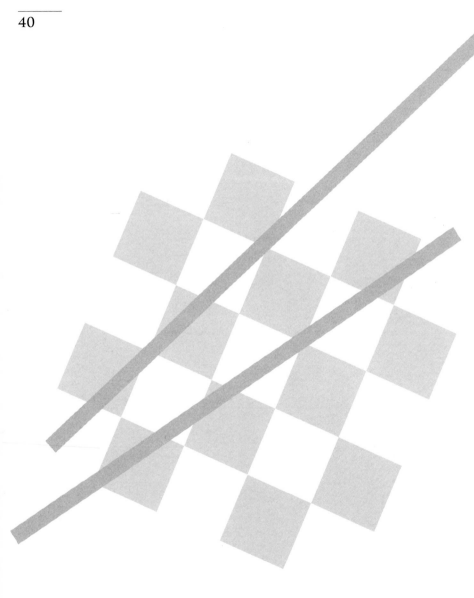

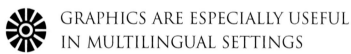

Donald McCarty designed the Education Sciences Building at the Madison campus of the University of Wisconsin. His final plan—a large central room with offices around the perimeter—closely resembled this one.

Informal Congregation Areas Are Essential

A healthy culture depends on its members' ability to gather together informally. In school, that often means gathering in bathrooms or crowded hallways, the library or media center. In effect, these locations become the family room of the school, so why not make them as inviting, easy to reach, and comfortable as our own family rooms? Such areas should have few visual boundaries and be centrally located, easily accessible, and on major traffic routes for all building users.

GRAPHICS ARE ESPECIALLY USEFUL IN MULTILINGUAL SETTINGS

It's particularly important in language-diverse settings for people to be able to communicate in ways other than speaking and writing. Over 50 percent of students in one urban school were from families newly settled in the United States. Children there enjoyed lunch box graphics on the cafeteria wall and murals of characters from children's books in the library. They and their parents could easily find the nurse's office with the big red cross on the door. The lavatories, designated by the international symbols for women and men, were obvious to everyone.

Some schools add stripes of contrasting color in floor tiles or on walls to be used as direction finders by first-time visitors. In addition to adding splash and a sense of joy to the building, graphics or an appropriate rebus painted on or attached to walls, doors, or floors help non-English-speaking users locate what they need and feel comfortable in the building.

The Outdoors Satisfies Several Needs

The importance of the outdoors is documented in almost every school. Visual accessibility to the outdoors and the choices available on the playground underscore the value of the outdoors to school users.

Being able to see what lies beyond the building's walls lets us know what's going on around us. It helps make life predictable for school users during an otherwise subject-segmented day. Students can see the milk truck delivering ice cream, a sibling having fun on the playground, the PE class playing softball on the field, or Mom as she arrives in the family car for volunteer lunch duty. Visual access

TO THE CONTRARY, PEOPLE WHO SHARE WORK SPACES OFTEN FORM COLLEGIAL RELATIONSHIPS AND HAVE A SENSE OF TEAM PLAY.

to the outdoors also allows minds and eyes to take a break. To be able to look up and out—to transport ourselves from the immediate to the imagined—gives us an essential restorative experience. Our sense of well-being is heightened when we view trees and shrubs.

The outdoors also supports people's preferences for personal choice. The outdoor area affords a wide array of choices in most schools. Tables and benches offer places to work puzzles, do math problems, play checkers, eat lunch, or read. Playground equipment offers children limitless opportunities to use their imaginations and make personal choices. Grassy fields can be appropriated for soccer, baseball, and football games or used as collection areas for science projects. What is most important is the variety actually *experienced* by users rather than the number of distinct activity settings available.

Multiple-Use Spaces Serve Many Purposes

Multiple-use spaces are often better than large numbers of individually assigned spaces. Areas within a building that are assigned (almost always by a higher authority) usually set up a formal, structured approach to the use of space. Staff members develop strong feelings of ownership for their assigned spaces: The art teacher might not want her room used by others because she doesn't want works in progress bothered; the kindergarten teacher resents extended-day children in his room after school because they don't return the crayons and other supplies to the right places; the music teacher is loathe to share her space because other teachers always rearrange her choir chairs.

To the contrary, people who share work spaces—and who are permitted to make their own work schedules—often form collegial relationships and have a sense of team play. In some schools where space is tight, working relationships are often characterized by spontaneity, a willingness to share, and flexibility. Everyone understands the problem of limited space and helps out by reordering schedules, relocating for a while, or changing planned activities. In other words, shared spaces act as a catalyst for focusing on the most important question—What's best for students?—instead of focusing on the possessive question—What belongs to me?

Successful mutual use of space seems to call into question the need for specialty areas that serve only one purpose—art, speech therapy, band, vocal music. Besides drawing staff members into more collegial relationships, reciprocity of space allows for smaller building size, eliminates redundant spaces, lowers the down-time of certain areas, and eliminates added costs that special-use areas often create.

• • •

These findings are, of course, specific to the schools I have studied. Like nationalities, religions, business organizations, families, or just about any group of people you can think of, each school has its own unique culture. That culture is a distillation from many years of users' experiences. And while an outsider may be perplexed by a particular culture's rituals, names, beliefs, or behaviors, insiders find them meaningful even when they're not able to clearly explain them.

Making these tacit meanings explicit enables those involved in designing buildings to create environments that support and enhance each culture.

Conversations with people from all walks of life have confirmed my belief that the surroundings in which we live, particularly the environments where we spent the majority of our growing-up time—our childhood homes and the schools we attended—have profound and lasting effects on our lives and learning.

School planners serious about creating facilities that inspire good teaching and support productive learning need to first study the cultural understandings of prospective users. Such cultural research allows for the creation of schools that really work for the people who inhabit them—meaningful places for teachers and students to carry out their daily living.

References

Bachelard, G. (1969). *The Poetics of Space*. Boston: Beacon Press. (First published as *La Poétique de L'Espace*, Presses Universitaires de France, 1958.)

Brenner, D. (September 1981). "A Meeting of Minds at Corning." *Architectural Record*, pp. 79–85.

Liebson, D.E. (September 1981). "How Corning Designed a 'Talking' Building to Spur Productivity." *Management Review*, pp. 8–13.

Schab, F.A. (1990). "Odors and the Remembrance of Things Past." *Journal of Experimental Psychology: Learning, Memory and Cognition* 16, 4: 648–655.

REVITALIZING AN OLDER SCHOOL

5

HAROLD L. HAWKINS

Jim McCormick knew it was time to do something. He had recently read about the potential of the physical environment to affect student learning and was now convinced that improving his school's environment could energize his students. Now beginning his fifth year as an elementary school principal—his second as principal of Oak Park Elementary—he felt it was time to establish himself, and his school, in the forefront of the growing emphasis on effective learning. The appropriate learning environment would certainly be a key to helping his students to greater learning.

Oak Park Elementary School* had 600 students in grades PreK–5. It had been built in the mid '70s, at a time when the Smithville community was experiencing rapid growth. The school building was the result of a rather hurried realization that even though tax monies were scarce, additional space was needed as quickly as possible. The building, when constructed, had been the best elementary school in the district. It was the only single-story elementary school; its corridors were 10 feet wide; and the classrooms were larger than those in other schools. Now, 20 years later, it was far from being a stimulating learning environment. Paint colors clashed and walls were badly marked

*The elementary school and the community cited here represent a composite of schools and communities I have known and worked with during my professional career.

up. There were no provisions for tack boards or display cases, which had been deleted from the original construction because of cost overruns.

McCormick sensed that focusing sharply on the relationship between the school facility and learning would require the right approach. In his experience, staff development programs had been sort of "ho-hum" affairs. In order to accomplish his vision of a transformed Oak Park, he would need strong personal interest on the part of all participants—teachers, aides, students, and parents. The 30-member teaching staff included several teachers who were responsible for implementing curricular changes and some others who were completing university commitments. As a principal, Jim was a realist when it came to developing teacher involvement; he knew those teachers were already deeply involved in other activities and weren't likely to be personally interested in or available for his visionary project. A group of 10 or 15 enthusiastic staffers would be more effective in demonstrating creative approaches to improving the physical learning environment than a larger group of "half-committed" participants. The third week in September seemed the best time to meet and discuss the learning environment project.

The day after Labor Day, McCormick distributed a memo to the staff about the project and his desire to improve the school's learning environment. The memo included two attachments: (1) *The Interface Profile* and (2) *The Interface Project's Teacher's Inventory of*

LOCAL HISTORY, ILLUSTRATED HERE BY A STUDENT-MADE QUILT, GIVES CHILDREN
A SENSE OF CONTINUITY WITH EARLY SETTLERS AND MAKES TEXTBOOK HISTORY
COME ALIVE.

Physical Learning Environment. The *Profile* presented six areas in which a school building can enhance the potential for student learning. The *Teacher's Inventory* was a brief instrument designed for rating the quality of a school's physical aspects. Interested staff members were asked to meet after school on Thursday of the following week to share their thoughts about the need to focus on the relationship between environment and learning.

"I'm pleased to see you're so interested in helping to create an improved learning environment here at Oak Park," McCormick told the small group who assembled for the meeting. "I know that the need to understand the link between learning potential and physical environment is not new to some of you. But it certainly has not been a major focus for us. I have noticed in recent months that many educational articles are discussing this topic. The two items attached to the memo announcing this meeting are a partial indication of new attitudes about the important role school buildings play in the educational program. I have other materials that I will also make available to you. Now let's hear your questions and comments."

After a slight pause, Geraldine Ferson, a 2nd grade teacher, opened the discussion. "I came to see what this proposal was all about," she said. "Although I'm in favor of doing whatever it takes to improve learning, right now seems like the wrong time to take on any more extra work."

The next reaction came from a second-year 5th grade teacher. "Our building is quite acceptable as it is, but I'm not sure," Henry Lowe offered, "that it does anything special to motivate teachers or students to do their best. However, I am in favor of doing anything we can to provide a better atmosphere for the teaching/learning process."

BRICK PLANTER WITH LIVING PLANTS CREATES A FOCAL POINT IN A LARGE LOBBY.

Juanita Garcia expressed her interest in the idea, but being a practical-minded professional, asked, "Are there any funds to get this thing started?"

An unpaid volunteer who worked two days a week in the school library ventured an opinion that window arrangements in the library tended to make the place seem dark and uninviting. She suggested that the PTA consider taking on a project to improve the general appearance of that area.

After another 20 minutes of discussion, Principal McCormick felt it was time to refocus. He wanted the group to have a basic understanding about the process of improving the learning environment. He reminded the group that the most significant decisions about how to create the best possible educational environment are

JUST WAITING FOR
WARM WEATHER,
THESE TABLES AND
BENCHES OFFER AN
INVITING SETTING FOR
OUTDOOR LEARNING
ACTIVITIES AND
PICNIC LUNCHES.

made when the building is designed and constructed. At that time, careful attention can be given to the way the interior and exterior are planned so as to best serve the instructional program, he told his staff. Limitations are, unfortunately, often built into the structure. He said the project that they were considering would be directed toward possible ways to make their existing 20-year-old building more attractive and enhance student learning.

To close the meeting, McCormick said he would be distributing within a few days information and a response form covering three aspects: (1) the opportunity to make a commitment to pursue improving the learning environment during the school year, (2) the selection of a preferred area of interest for study and implementation, and (3) the identification of students, parents, and others who might be willing to assist in the endeavor.

McCormick's follow-up memo also mentioned that the *Interface Profile* provided a broad overview of how a *total* building might better contribute to learning. He suggested that to be most efficient, the planning group should concentrate on three focal points: building exterior, corridors and foyers, and flexible room arrangements. Subcommittees would be needed for each. In addition to the response form, McCormick also attached a bibliography of materials available in the teachers' professional library that were related to learning environments.

The memo also explained that much could be accomplished without specific funding; for example, room arrangements, new pictures, and use of plants. For major needs, such as corridor benches and outdoor work, the administration was willing to provide some financial assistance.

The response forms were due back in one week and the group would reconvene in two weeks to consider if the project was a "go" or not.

McCormick studied the responses during the next week after they were compiled. All but one person from the initial group responded positively, and three additional teachers volunteered to get involved. Seven staffers wanted to work on flexible room arrangements. Corridors and foyers attracted the interest of five individuals, with a chairperson yet to be identified. Juanita Garcia, sensing where some funding might be available, signed up along with two others for the building exterior. She expressed a willingness to head that group, which also included several older students and five parent volunteers. McCormick hoped one of those parents, an architect with some experience in educational facilities, would agree to lead the corridors and foyers group.

When the nearly 25 group members met the following week, everyone expressed very real enthusiasm for the project. McCormick added his appreciation for the level of involvement thus far. Several of the teachers had retrieved articles from the teachers' library and they shared their findings with the others.

Juanita Garcia had read material from the Council of Educational Facility Planners, including their Strategic Plan. "I found two of their new belief statements to be very compelling," she reported. "They state: '(1) There is an integral relationship between the quality of education and the quality of educational facilities, and (2) Every student deserves a clear, safe, comfortable, and pleasant environment in which to learn.' I believe," Garcia continued, "that what

NOOKS AND CRANNIES AND BEANBAG CHAIRS FOSTER THE USE OF IMAGI-
NATION AND CREATE SMALL OASES OF PRIVACY WITHIN BUSY SPACES.

we are about to do here at Oak Park Elementary can really make a difference in how students learn. After all, the real test of a good environment is if people are there when they don't have to be. A more pleasing school environment will perhaps help to keep students and teachers in the building longer and be more effective in their work."

McCormick then laid out some guidelines for how the project would proceed. "We will not hold a lot of meetings," he said. "Each of the topic groups will have considerable autonomy. I encourage your subcommittees to consider these directions: (1) Continue to review the literature on learning environments. (2) Add members to your groups to the extent possible. (3) Include students in your activities. (4) Encourage teachers on an individual basis to use the *Teacher's Inventory of Physical Learning Environment*. (5) Begin soon to develop lists of desirable improvements. (6) When your lists are fully developed, select the ideas that seem manageable and include estimates of costs where outside funds might be needed. (7) Be ready for a review and discussion meeting with our total group in six weeks."

Having provided some direction, the principal then adjourned the meeting. He felt that the demonstration project would produce some beneficial results for students and teachers alike.

Two weeks before the next scheduled meeting in early November, McCormick distributed a reminder for that session. He also asked each of the three subcommittees to prepare a list of three to five suggestions for improving the learning environment. Enthusiasm continued to build and several times before the next meeting, team members stopped by McCormick's office to raise questions about various ideas their groups were considering. When everyone assembled for that meeting, several parents and about a dozen older students were also in attendance. The air was charged with anticipation and high expectations. Students exhibited an enthusiasm that came from a new belief that their school was undergoing a change. Teachers who had felt the satisfaction of decorating and improving their own homes now had a similar sense that their "work home" also was undergoing a renewal.

The Building Exterior group presented its plan first, followed by the Corridors and Foyers group. Their summaries of modifications and cost estimates are shown in Figures 5.1 and 5.2. Both reports were received favorably. McCormick then called for the Flexible Room Arrangements report.

Henry Lowe, Flexible Room Arrangements group chair, made some comments prior to distributing that group's report. "Our meetings started with little expectation that much change was possible. We knew our rooms had less space than desirable for today's

FIGURE 5.1
PROPOSED IMPROVEMENTS TO
BUILDING EXTERIOR

SUGGESTION	SOURCE	COST
1. Install four concrete benches near front entrance where the Bradford pear trees were planted last year	Assistance from district Maintenance Department	$400
2. Provide six raised planters (landscape timbers) on slab near Early Elementary wing on existing cement slab; can be used for student garden projects	Assembled by the PTA Fathers Club	$0
3. Provide shrubbery across main front section of the building (mixture of hawthorn and roses)	Local nursery will provide at cost; planting by high school science class	$500
4. Provide five new picnic tables at the rear of the building; to be used by students with bag lunches and for outdoor classes	To be constructed by high school wood shop classes	$500

TOTAL: $1,400

FIGURE 5.2
PROPOSED IMPROVEMENTS TO
CORRIDORS AND FOYERS

SUGGESTION	SOURCE	COST
1. Historical quilted wall hanging for entrance wall	Identify persons to quilt blocks based on community history	$0
2. Historical school furniture representing early days of Smithville placed under open corridor stairway area	Obtain assistance of the Smithville Community Historical Association for furniture and pictures	$0
3. To improve environment, provide round table, chair, bench, and plants to be placed in the main front corridor	Order to be placed through Purchasing Department	$2,000 To be shared equally by the school system and PTA
4. Provide new brick planter to be placed near the front entrance; also provide a new brick planter (10' circumference) placed adjacent to the Principal's office	Architect member of the committee to design the planters; brick to match building interior exposed brick	Brick construction estimated at $1000 and $300 cost of greenery to be from Oak Park Elem. School Discretionary Fund
		TOTAL: $3,300

FIGURE 5.3
GUIDELINES FOR FLEXIBLE
ROOM ARRANGEMENTS

1
Arrange furniture to permit group activities and easy movement of teachers and students.

2
Use alcove arrangements for interest centers, individual student withdrawal space, and access to computers.

3
Add color in rooms through tack boards and psychologically effective wall paint.

4
Add displays of greenery in each room.

5
Remove furniture, materials, and equipment not in regular use.

curriculum. Then several of us used the *Teacher's Inventory*. To our surprise, we found that many variations on room arrangements are possible. Our report differs from the ones already presented because we believe that funding is not as important as really discovering what each room contains and how a specific room needs to function.

So we wrote our report to provide some basic guidelines for flexible room arrangements" (Figure 5.3).

After the three groups had reported, Principal McCormick discussed the possible cost of the combined projects:

Amount	Source
$ 300	Oak Park Elementary School Discretionary Fund
1,000	PTA
3,400	School District
$4,700	Total cash needed for all projects

The group was excited about how the plans would affect the appearance of their 20-year-old building. McCormick thanked all three groups for their imaginative efforts and went on to emphasize the potential of their recommendations to positively improve students' learning. "Oak Park may not be new," he said, "but we can make it a showplace for learning with the plans presented here today. I'm giving you the green light to proceed!"

McCormick concluded the meeting by offering a suggestion from his readings on school facility planning. "We need to share our thinking and our plans with all students, parents, and the community. Let's begin right now to plan a School Building Day for next April.

GREEN PLANTS, ACCESSIBLE FURNITURE, AND INTERESTING ARTWORK MAKE THE LIBRARY HOMELIKE AND INVITING

Our staff and students can lead the way in placing a new emphasis on the importance of the school building," he said. "And our actions can help our community understand that a quality physical environment is essential to effective learning."

WORDS BY ANNE MEEK

PHOTOGRAPHS BY
STEVEN LANDFRIED

CROW ISLAND SCHOOL: 54 YEARS YOUNG

6

You walk toward the front door of Crow Island School, through the plaza where the children arrive each morning, and you're not sure what's familiar and what's not. Crow Island is different, but not all that different, at first.

The plaza is both familiar and unfamiliar. You've seen many school loading zones, of course; but this one's wide, rounded lines seem to gather youngsters in, welcoming them, protecting them, even hugging them. And the broad steps with short risers are inviting, making it look easy and natural to trip right on up the steps to school.

But the tower is not familiar. Tall and imposing, it contrasts the open arms of the plaza. Your eye can't just skip over that tower—and imagine what you would think if you were a person standing only three or four feet tall. That tower would tell you: *This is not an ordinary place . . . Something very important is going on here . . . It's all right to build towers . . . that's what people do . . . So what tower are you going to build?*

This message could be frightening—it's a challenge—but then you see the clock. Set askew on the tower, in the most unpredictable

perch, the clock lets you know this is a place for surprises, too. The clock tells you not to take yourself too seriously: *We can have a lot of fun here . . . finding things that aren't where we expect them to be and trying out ideas of our own about where things can be.*

Then you're at the front door, and what you notice is that the door handle is too low. Too low for you, just right for children.

Oh. It's a place for children.

Then you're inside, and the mystery is still there, the blurring of familiar and unfamiliar. But

you forget the mystery: children fill the hallways, there are hand rails at three levels to accommodate their varied heights, the walls are sturdy, the whole place looks durable and safe, comfortable and accepting.

Open the door to a Crow Island classroom, and you're in familiar territory. It's unmistakably a classroom, yet it's a living room, with windows, books, and a rug. No, it's a workshop, with a sink, a work table, stacks of materials, and busy people everywhere you look. Groups of desks and chairs appear here and there. Crayon drawings and torn-paper collages adorn the pine-panelled walls in no particular pattern. Children sit, walk, are up on their knees in their chairs; they talk, retrieve dropped pencils, study, and ask questions.

And sometimes they look out the windows to the courtyard and beyond, to the woods, pondering a puzzling idea, imagining, or just daydreaming.

 COLLABORATIVE
ARCHITECTURAL PLANNING

You start to take a closer look, interested now in why it's so right. How did Crow Island happen? How is it that, even now, in its 54th year of service, Crow Island School is still going strong, when, by most accounts, the life span of a school building is 50 years? Here, teachers like their classrooms, busy youngsters feel they belong, and the community points with pride to its school, now a national landmark.

It all began in 1919 when the Winnetka, Illinois, school board, bent on reform, hired Carleton Washburne as superintendent. An energetic young teacher from San Francisco, Washburne was on fire to break up the lockstep approach to teaching and to create activity-based programs of learning.

Once in Winnetka—his superintendency spanned 24 years—Washburne established a continuous progress curriculum to ensure mastery of basic skills, along with attention to social development, creative activities, and experiential learning (Pick 1991, p. 18).

In 1937, the board began once again to consider construction projects, long delayed by the Depression. Soon, Larry Perkins, a young architect who wanted the "Northwest School" job, arranged an interview with the superintendent. Washburne set forth high expectations:

> This is to be our dream school. For years we have been thinking about it.
> We want it to be the most functional and beautiful school in the world.
> We want it to crystallize in architecture the best of our educational thought
> and to house appropriately the educational practices we can evolve (Pick
> 1991, p. 1).

Washburne was not sure Perkins possessed the necessary prowess for such a vision; he suggested collaboration with a "great architect." Perkins pressed for a name. Washburne named Eliel Saarinen, whose first American work was Cranbrook, a girls' school outside Detroit. So Perkins, in a wild gamble, promised to obtain the services of the eminent Finnish architect.

And Perkins did just that, although he himself took the responsibility for achieving harmony between education and architecture, leaving the design direction to Saarinen and to his son Eero, who joined the project a little later.

To ensure harmony between the structure and the curriculum, Perkins went back to school, sitting in classrooms to understand what went on and how to house it. He solicited suggestions from teachers, parents, custodians, and the children. Eventually, before the overall plan was drawn, he built a cardboard model of the L-shaped classroom, the design emerging from his synthesis of the suggestions. This model was then carried from place to place, meeting to meeting, and everyone commented, wondered aloud, and offered more ideas.

These "contributing designers" were clear: They wanted a building built to the scale of children and an environment that promoted a sense of belonging, of community. They did not want a building to convey unreality, some palace of childish delights. That would send the wrong message. Frances Presler, then director of activities for the school, set down the important ideas in a letter to the architects.

> Above all, the school must be childlike—not what adults think of children. At the same time it should be dignified, and playful, but not a playing down to children. It must be a place for living, a place for use, good hard use, for it is to be successively the home, the abiding place for a procession of thousands of children through the years. It must be warm, personal, and intimate, that it shall be to each of these thousands "my school."

> The school should look to the future. It should not seem complete and finished beyond any addition or adjustment to later demands. It should give children and adults the feeling of flexibility, possibility of change . . . (Presler 1941).

A PLACE FOR CHILDREN

How, then, to account for 50+ years of vitality? Of course, there are the visionary leaders to thank, the collaborative planning to acknowledge, and the support of a close-knit community to recognize—all attributes of success in achieving good schools. Ah, but more than anything else, this school works because it's a good place for children to live and learn as they journey from their nursery-homes toward the larger world.

Educational thought and practice change often, but childhood itself is not a fad or fashion. Despite new knowledge and new ideas, children continue to encounter the daily demands of growth and development, demands that are remarkably resistant to change. These daily demands translate into life tasks that include matters of identity, both personal and cultural, relationships with self and others, and evolving mastery of the environments in which children find themselves. There is simply no other way to grow up except by facing and surviving, and perhaps achieving well, these daily demands.

The messages—aesthetic and social—of Crow Island School support the work of childhood, of achieving well the life tasks of growing up. This structure says to children: *The world around you is* *durable and safe . . . It is the dwelling place of the human family . . . You are a cherished member of that family . . . You have a part in it . . . Your part calls for honest responses, joyful effort, and thoughtful contributions.* These are the messages that children everywhere need to see and hear.

References

Pick, G. (March 1, 1991). "A School Fit for Children." *Reader* (Chicago's Free Weekly) 20, 21: 1, 14, 16, 18–26.

Presler, Frances. (1941). "A Letter to the Architects." In *Crow Island School, Winnetka, Ill.*, reprinted from *The Architectural Forum*, August 1941.

PLANNING YOUR SCHOOL'S TECHNOLOGY FUTURE

7

BOB VALIANT

Improving school learning environments requires careful consideration of a wide range of issues, as outlined in the table of contents of this book. Leading-edge planners recognize the increasingly important role technology will play in schools and thus incorporate and coordinate plans for technology into their facility planning efforts. This chapter provides a framework for conceptualizing technology systems that are consistent with instructional philosophy, management needs, and overall facility design.

Every technology planning effort is different. The people involved have individual levels of knowledge and interest, existing conditions vary from place to place, and expectations and purposes result in alternative design solutions. In fact, nearly all aspects of technology as applied to education are in a state of flux.

Given the complexity of the situation, it's important that you do all you can to ensure that the design of infrastructure, systems, and other components of applied technology meet your educational requirements now and in the future. In striving to develop a suitable technology plan within your budget, your ultimate goal should be to design a flexible system that will allow growth as resources become available and as technology continues its rapid, inexorable transmutations. Accomplishing this important task requires that you look at several questions regarding how you will gather and analyze data, set criteria, examine alternatives, and make decisions about technology.

WHERE ARE YOU NOW?

Before beginning any technology planning effort, you must assess where you are now and identify the resources you can provide and the needs you foresee. A technology planning team, tied closely to the facility planning effort, should be formed early in the planning process to handle this and other such questions. Hiring an outside facilitator with planning and technology expertise is helpful in most cases. Your technology planning team should include representatives of various technology user groups and might consist of the principal, teachers, a media specialist, a school secretary, and other support staff. Parents and older students can also add to the team. Current knowledge, interest in technology, and stature with peers are criteria that can be used during team member selection.

A formal linkage, with periodic reporting, must be established between the technology team and the overall facility design group. Your architect or other members of the facility design team might even wish to be included in development of the technology plan. Be sure to identify all such stakeholders early in the process.

Once formed, the team should complete a thorough needs assessment. The first component of the needs assessment should be an inventory of currently owned equipment (with details about the numbers of items, their age, reliability, and so on) and a detailed study of currently owned software. Existing networking capabilities and descriptions of current delivery systems for print and other

PARENTS, COMMUNITY MEMBERS, AND TALENTED STUDENTS MAY HAVE EXACTLY THE EXPERTISE YOU REQUIRE.

media should also be carefully described. Collaboration with building or district curriculum planners will help the technology committee understand the school programs they need to serve.

A second important, but often neglected, portion of the needs assessment is the training and interest level of building staff. The best building technology plan will fail if staff does not know how to use the installed system, or if they refuse to use it. Early identification of problems in this area can help the planning team focus on solutions.

A third component of the needs assessment is identification of resources. Outside consultants with specific expertise are available to help your team (see the list at the end of this chapter). Your state education agency is usually a good source of references and might even offer assistance itself. Professional organizations such as ASCD, the Council of Educational Facility Planners, and the International Society for Technology in Education provide workshops, seminars, and printed materials that can aid your planning team. And be sure not to overlook the help that is close at hand. Parents, community members, and talented students may have exactly the expertise you require.

Partnerships with local businesses have also proven helpful in schools where the concept has been explored.

An honest appraisal of financial resources should also be attempted by the planning team. Current funding levels for technology, bonding capacity, special levies, grants, partnerships, and fundraisers are topics others have explored with varying degrees of success.

WHAT DO YOU HOPE TO ACHIEVE?

Having a carefully crafted sense of your needs and resources helps set the stage for your next task, determining the purposes your technology plan will address. Statements such as "We want to be number one in technology" might be helpful, but are not sufficient. Planning teams often begin their quest with such broad vision statements and then spend much of their "visioning" time on state-of-the-art equipment and software. It may be more useful to try to picture what people will be doing in schools in 5, 10, and 20 years and then to describe how they will be using technology in the various time periods. We know, for example, that there is a trend toward more project-centered learning with flexible student groupings. Try to picture what that will look like in action.

It might also be useful at this point to call in outside consultants to help your committee create a vision of the future of educa-

tion. Harold Shane, Marvin Cetron, and others have written popular books on this topic, and ASCD's *Educational Leadership* has carried a number of articles that can help you as you begin. The ASCD Educational Futurists Network is another good place to go for help.

Technology applications center around three primary systems: instruction, management, and communication. A useful exercise for the planning team is to describe what people will be doing within each system 5, 10, and 20 years in the future. For example, as you walk through a school in 10 years, what adults do you see in the instructional program, and what are they doing? Are they all teachers, or are some parents, community volunteers, senior citizens, or business people? Are they talking to children, assisting them, reading, preparing material? How are they using technology in each of these tasks? The same process should be repeated regarding what is happening with children. How they are grouped, the materials they are working with, and the activities they are pursuing should all be described, and technology applications should be noted.

Continue the process for management and communication systems. In the end, a matrix showing expected technology applica-

HAVING A CAREFULLY CRAFTED SENSE OF YOUR NEEDS AND RESOURCES HELPS SET THE STAGE FOR YOUR NEXT TASK,

tions in each of the systems during each time period can be teased out of the narratives to focus attention on what you want to eventually be able to do with technology in your school.

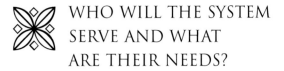

WHO WILL THE SYSTEM SERVE AND WHAT ARE THEIR NEEDS?

Potential users of technology in the school include students, teachers, administration, and support staff. Additionally, because it is now common to design spaces in schools that can be utilized by community agencies, parents, and other citizens, the needs of these groups should also be considered.

Students should, of course, be the primary users of technology at the school site. Traditional uses include computer-aided instruction (from workbook style exercises to simulation of real events), word processing, and spreadsheet and data processing programs. The current trend is toward combining two or more of these activities as students work in teams to produce new knowledge. Information for these projects can be obtained from books, CD-ROM disks, or interactive sources from around the world. One of the critical decisions your planning team will need to make concerns how much of this vast network will be made available in the classroom and how much will require students to go to the library, computer center, or elsewhere.

TEACHERS WILL PLAY A KEY ROLE IN TECHNOLOGY IMPLEMENTATION AND USE AND SHOULD BE INVOLVED IN ALL PHASES OF YOUR PLAN'S DEVELOPMENT.

Another major area of student involvement with technology is in learning how it works and what can be done with it. Technology education now includes such topics as principles of technology, material science, computer-aided drafting and design, robotics, and programming. Each of these applications has facility design implications and should be considered in your plan.

Teachers will play a key role in technology implementation and use and should be involved in all phases of your plan's development. Teachers will be involved in all three components of your technology system. They will facilitate learning through application of the instructional components and will, in many cases, participate as coworkers with students in knowledge production activities.

Administrative functions include typical information gathering and storage, and networks between classrooms and administration, counseling, and registration offices. Energy use and security are examples of administrative areas with potential for technological assistance. Districtwide networks of these and other administrative functions should be considered as you plan.

Support staff must also be considered when planning for technology use. The library or media center can make use of all three systems described above: instructional support can be provided through services originating in the media center and transmitted throughout the building over cables; students can be brought to the center or cart-based units can be distributed for use in individual work spaces; and automated check-out systems can facilitate resource management while communication with the classrooms and online resources open the world to students.

One of the difficulties of implementing any change of this magnitude is the uneven training of the people expected to carry it out. Some teachers, administrators, and students will be on the cutting edge of technology while others will exhibit trepidation at the mere thought of having to change. Include careful consideration of training needs and ongoing support of the staff in your deliberations.

Community use of technology owned by the school also deserves consideration. Many districts house public agencies, day care, and senior citizen facilities on school premises. Community recreation is another frequent user of classrooms and gyms. Technology can play an important role for each of these potential tenants and their advice should be sought as you create your technology plan.

Communication needs raise the question of accessibility of telephones. Many technology planning teams have concluded that each classroom, office, and work space in a school should be equipped with telephones with outside access. Teachers, of course, will also need access to telephones for internal communication with each other and the administration. Appropriate use of technology has the potential to bring the school and the home closer together. Homework hotlines and parent bulletin boards are two examples of this kind of application that your planning team should consider.

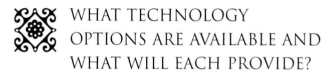 ## WHAT TECHNOLOGY OPTIONS ARE AVAILABLE AND WHAT WILL EACH PROVIDE?

Most of the current technological base in school buildings is made up of stand-alone equipment designed for a specific use and assigned to a particular space. Networks, where they exist, are usually found in computer labs and administrative offices. Few bridges exist to tie together these various applications. Your planning team should consider the many technologies that exist and what they provide that might be useful in your situation. Team members will need to decide which technology options are suited to your school's needs and whether or not they will be interconnected.

Growing numbers of individual personal computers are available in schools everywhere. As stand-alone devices, they provide a platform for word processing, data processing, and spreadsheet development and can be used with various forms of computer-aided and computer-managed learning. With the addition of peripherals,

SCHOOLS
DESIGNED
TO LAST
40 YEARS OR
MORE MUST
INCLUDE AT
LEAST THE
INFRASTRUC-
TURE TO
MAKE THIS
INTERCON-
NECTIVITY
POSSIBLE.

these devices enable communication with distant sources of information, creation of multimedia presentations, and publication of complex documents. If only one computer is available in a classroom, it may be used as a "learning center" where students take turns using it as part of a learning sequence.

Computer labs provide all of the advantages of stand-alone personal computers with the addition of the savings of network licenses for software. Entire classes can be brought together for group instruction or project work. Disadvantages include the need to move students from their normal work spaces, scheduling difficulties, supervision, and maintenance.

The addition of telephones, VCRs, fax machines, projection devices, and interactive laser discs increases the usefulness of a technology system in libraries, offices, labs, and classrooms. Many districts are now establishing interconnections among all of the technologies within and between schools. Distant sources can be brought into the building on phone lines, wide area network cabling, satellite dishes, and so forth. If several networked stations are envisioned for each teach-

ing station, furniture requirements and space allocation also become significant issues for consideration. The flexibility these plans provide comes with a price, of course. But many people argue that schools designed to last 40 years or more must include at least the infrastructure to make this interconnectivity possible.

 ## HOW CAN YOU GUARD AGAINST OBSOLESCENCE?

There are no guarantees, of course. Technology is advancing at a rapid pace, and new developments seem to pour out in a never-ending stream. Many schools are trying to stay ahead of the wave by installing large cable trays throughout their campuses. This assumes that buildingwide networks will continue to be carried on cables of some sort into the near future, which most experts agree is likely for video/data networks because of the bandwidth required for video signals.

Other decisions about future use are a bit tougher to make. The present solution (with likely viability of more than 10 years) is fiber-optic cable. Installation of such a system allows for handling known networking requirements with room for expansion as new applications develop. The cost of such a system is dropping rapidly, and many schools are providing several pairs of fiber in the cable trays for each work space throughout each building, which may or may not be connected to devices at the ends of the cable. Because it is cheaper to pull the cable before ceilings are installed, this is some-times done even if terminators and other devices are not yet in the budget.

Most experts recommend installing a system designed to carry video on a data network with at least the capabilities of Category 5 twisted-pair copper. This cable option appears to meet the needs of most current applications and those likely to be used in the next 10 or so years. It is less expensive than the fiber option but does not provide as safe a cushion for future development.

Wherever possible, it is recommended that telephone lines be provided to each work space in a school. Outside lines are usually brought into a digital PBX. Voice mail and connections to the video/data network for zonal paging should also be considered. All of this equipment plus file servers, CD-ROM towers, and so forth require space. Head-end equipment is usually located in a room near the media center or office, but closets may also be required at strategic locations throughout large buildings.

WHAT WILL IT COST?

Planning groups must consider at least five cost centers as they pre-pare estimates for installation and operation of technology systems. Staff development costs are often underestimated or even ignored in the planning process. These costs begin, however, with the training of the planning committee and continue through full implementa-tion and beyond. If a continuous improvement model is used, expect these costs to peak during the first three years, but to persist into the future as new people are hired and advanced systems are introduced.

Infrastructure and hardware are two obvious cost centers and require careful consideration. Infrastructure decisions must be made early in the planning process because size and placement affect facil-ity structure and mechanical and electrical systems. Technology sys-tems, including hardware decisions, should be delayed as long as possible to ensure that the most current equipment is considered for installation. In the rapidly changing environment of technology applications, it is wise to purchase equipment at the latest possible date to meet school opening requirements.

Software and courseware, while not directly associated with school construction, are a significant part of the budget for making your technology system operational. A part of your planning group should be charged early on with the task of selecting these materials, but decisions ought to be delayed until equipment has been selected to ensure compatibility.

A final cost, also often overlooked, is the continuing cost of system support. Maintenance of equipment, network management, and personnel to operate certain systems are major elements of effective technology use. Permanent district staff are usually assigned to these tasks, but, under some conditions, using outside services can be financially advantageous. Cost, reliability, and timeliness of service should be factors in your planning team's decision.

 WHERE CAN YOU
FIND HELP?

Good news! Help abounds. State agencies, organizations, and publications—each provides a different type of information. Some especially useful sources of help follow. Perhaps the best advice comes from Rich Hug, technology coordinator in the Carterville, Georgia, schools. Rich says, "Ask questions, ask questions, ask questions!"   Many districts now staff technology positions, and people love to tell you what they know. Learn from other districts' successes and failures, and get a wide cross section of opinions. If possible, identify schools and districts with similar goals and take your planning team, armed with questions, for a visit. What you learn may save a lot of aggravation and will certainly contribute to the successful completion of your facility technology plan.

Resources

Organizations

Association for Supervision and Curriculum Development
1250 N. Pitt Street
Alexandria, VA 22314-1403
(703) 549-9110
Resources: Education and Technology Resources Center, print materials.

Council of Educational Facility Planners International
8687 E. Via de Ventura, Suite 311
Phoenix, AZ 85258-3347
(602) 948-2337
Resources: Annual seminar, print materials, consultant listing.

International Society for Technology in Education
1787 Agate
Eugene, OR 97403-1923
(503) 346-4414
Resources: Print materials, conferences.

International Technology Education Association
1914 Association Drive
Reston, VA 22091
(703) 860-2100
Resources: Print materials, videos, technology bank.

State and Regional Education Agencies
Resources: Varies, but most states now provide staff to assist districts with their technology planning efforts.

Equipment Vendors

Resources: Virtually all equipment vendors provide staff to help with technology planning. Be aware that they are selling as well as helping. Technical documents and catalogs are useful.

Books

Microcomputer Facilities in School by L.J. Espinoza. (Englewood, Colo.: Libraries Unlimited, Inc., 1990.) Now somewhat dated, but still useful as a planning tool.

Multimedia and Learning: A School Leader's Guide, edited by A.W. Ward. (Alexandria, Va.: National School Boards Association, 1994.) A nontechnical guide to multimedia education. Includes a brief chapter on facility planning for multimedia education.

Newton's Telecom Dictionary by H. Newton. (New York: Telecom Library, Inc., 1993.) A glossary of telecommunications and voice-processing terms.

Retrofit for Technology Project: Technical Guidelines. (Tallahassee: Florida Department of Education, Office of Educational Technology, 1993.) A useful technical description of various communications distribution systems.

Periodicals

T.H.E. Journal, Electronic Learning, and *Technology and Learning.* These journals will help keep you current.

Curriculum/Technology Quarterly, a newsletter of the Association for Supervision and Curriculum Development.

ARCHITECTURE AND THE
STUDY OF THE BUILT
ENVIRONMENT SYNTHESIZE
THE WORLD OF IDEAS
AND THE WORLD OF
MATERIAL THINGS.

—ANNE TAYLOR

HOW SCHOOLS ARE REDESIGNING THEIR SPACE

8

ANNE TAYLOR

Children work in a solar greenhouse, graphing plant growth, classifying and comparing types of plants, and harvesting food and flowers. They learn about physics from the structure of the building, and they investigate the visible electrical–mechanical system to learn about input and output systems similar to the arteries and veins in their bodies. The problems they study in this "classroom" are real-world efforts, not bits of abstract work. Rather than completing worksheets, students participate in the concrete experiences that underlie mathematics, engineering, science, social studies, and art.

This greenhouse is one example of the indoor and outdoor learning environments that architect George Vlastos and I have been planning and designing for 20 years. We have come to think of educational architecture as a "three-dimensional textbook," a learning environment that is a functional art form, a place of beauty, and a motivational center for learning. We use the architecture of the school classroom, museum exhibits, and the landscape to demonstrate how the natural and built environments reveal the ideas, laws, and principles that we are trying to teach children from textbooks.

We believe that architectural settings can stimulate or subdue learning, aid creativity or slow mental perception. School restructuring efforts have not, however, addressed the physical learning environment as a support system for education. While trying to improve the quality of education with new curriculums, technologies, and strategies, educators and policymakers must not forget the structures and spaces where our children go to school.

RETHINKING SCHOOL ARCHITECTURE

The current revolution in education demands that we rethink the architecture that houses our children. To accommodate new teaching styles such as interdisciplinary and team teaching, schools need updated classrooms. They need technology studios, outdoor ecological landscapes, spaces for the arts, teaching museums, and flexible furniture systems and designs to meet the needs of students with disabilities. New environments are also needed to foster lifelong learning, preschool through old age.

Yet 50 percent of U.S. school buildings were constructed cheaply and rapidly in the 1950s and 1960s, built as if architects used cookie cutters to create classrooms, hallways, and cafeterias. Many schools need major repairs, contain environmental hazards, or exceed their planned capacity. The playground, perhaps the most valuable piece of real estate in the neighborhood, has been forgotten, left a barren patch of ground.

BY BEING COGNIZANT OF THE DESIGNED OR NATURAL WORLD, EDUCATORS CAN TURN "THINGS" INTO "THOUGHTS" FOR CHILDREN.

Because architecture can facilitate the transmission of cultural values, we need to look at what our present school buildings are saying to our children. We expect schools to prepare children for living in a democratic society, yet we provide a learning environment that resembles a police state—hard, overly durable architecture, giant chain-link fences, locked gates, guards, and even guard dogs.

An architect who had been designing prisons in a large city recently asked a colleague to examine a few of his school designs. There was a distinct similarity. Such architecture fails to encourage the sense of ownership, participation, or responsibility required for a democracy. Students are not prisoners who need surveillance, but children who need freedom to grow. What kinds of learning environments will support the education our children need?

New discoveries document that children learn best in stimulating and varied physical environments (Taylor and Vlastos 1983). In a recent journal article, the Council for Education Facility Planners International (1995) cited findings from a Washington, D.C., study in which the standardized test scores of students who were assigned to schools that were in poor physical condition fell 5.5 percent below those in fair condition and 11 percent below those in excellent condition. The U.S. Department of Education estimates that 90 million adults in America are functionally illiterate. Each year, private business spends $30 billion on worker training and loses $25–30 billion as a result of poor literacy among workers. The quality of the environment can either hinder or help learning. To short- change our children by housing them in buildings or in poorly designed portables, which we as adults would shun, is almost the crime of the century. Howard Gardner's (1983) work on multiple intelligences demonstrates that children need learning environments that facilitate a wide variety of access to knowledge and its application; Gardner recommends that schools be designed as museums to accommodate the diversity of learning styles.

Science and children's museums are our most successful contemporary learning environments. Geared to multisensory and interactive learning, they house enticing realia with appropriate autotelic exhibits and cases. Schools, too, could provide similar spaces. For example, science departments, instead of storing equipment and specimens in closets, could display these learning tools as part of a school or hallway science museum.

The architectural world surrounding us has wondrous messages. By being cognizant of the designed or natural world, educators can turn "things" into "thoughts" for children. Many schools complain that they cannot afford the manipulatives or materials to better teach mathematics and science, but even the school environ-

QUIET, INEXPENSIVE, MOVEABLE SEATS ACCOMMODATE GROUPWORK, CONFERENCES,
AND FRIENDSHIPS IN AN INVITING COMMONS.

ment—the buildings, the trees, the dirt, and the grass—can become
convenient teaching tools for innovative educators.

Architects who are alert to educational goals and the myriad
range of design possibilities can help to marry the world of education with the world of architecture when designing new schools.

Using ideas such as Gardner's multiple intelligences can make the
learning environment an active—not passive—set of spaces. In this
way, school facilities become a value-driven design.

 ## ARCHITECTURAL PROGRAMMING

One of the problems in building or renovating schools to reflect the
new theories in education is that planners rarely consult the users of
the space—the students, the teachers, the parents, and the community. To ensure effective communication among all who will eventually use a new or renovated school, we employ a planning process
called *architectural programming*. Before beginning the architectural
design phase, educators, planners, students, and community members can systematically discuss and then transform their mission and
objectives into activity settings. The process enables the planners to
identify program elements (not just square footage and dimensions)
as educational specifications, correlate them with academic curriculum content in a "Program for Design," and incorporate the program
into the final design for the school building and site.

Typically, we ask the community and those who will occupy
the building for information about what the new building requires;
we study the students and teachers, their special needs and aesthetic
preferences, and the spaces required. We find design determinants
in the children's developmental needs, likes, dislikes, and ideas
about learning, as well as in the curriculum content. We also look at

that is, how goals for the learners can be translated into architecture so the resulting environment is a true learning environment.

4. Test the concepts—will they work? Sketch them out. What learning implications do they have? How do they reflect the goals?

5. Ask more questions. What other needs does the client have? Is anything indispensable? What creative new ideas will support the goals and concepts? What innovative space concepts are available to meet the goals?

6. Define and solve the problems with design alternatives and concepts.

community resources available for education. The following steps summarize the data-gathering process (Pena 1987, Taylor 1995):

1. Establish goals by examining curriculum and the developmental needs of the target population. (Make sure users are included on the design team.)

2. Collect and analyze all facts, including climate, geography, community priorities, and all information from Step 1.

3. Determine how "things can be translated into thoughts"—

 ## REDESIGNING A HEAD START CLASSROOM

A few years ago we used architectural programming with Head Start teachers in New Mexico to design the "Head Start Classroom of the Future" (Taylor et al. 1989–92). We analyzed 14 typical early childhood learning zones and their relationships to one another,

to teaching concepts, and to learning processes. From this analysis, we devised a classroom that opens, closes up, and moves around, providing a way for teachers and children to set up a particular learning environment anywhere.

The new system includes several modular interdisciplinary pavilions: a design studio for drawing and painting; a spatial relationship environment for construction, movement, music, drama, and cognitive skill development; a garden; a portable cooking center; a media center with computer and audiovisual instruments; a "nest" —a soft, flexible environment with subdued color, texture, and sound, for listening and role-playing; a showcase environment for drawing, creative dramatics, and learning about light, color, reflection, and refraction; and a trash management center for developing ecological understanding. The flexibility of the environments provides an important tool for interdisciplinary teaching and for facilitating self-selection among the users.

 # DESIGNING FOR CULTURAL DIVERSITY

In designing our Head Start classroom, we discovered that different cultures have different spatial needs. For example, the Native American teachers in our group preferred rounded forms over rectilinear rooms. As we examined how to better use the corners of rooms, which often hold only unused junk, these teachers wanted

STUDENTS IN AN
ELEMENTARY SCHOOL IN
NEW MEXICO DESIGNED
AND PAINTED THEIR
MURAL, WITH THE HELP
OF AN ARTIST.

to store toys and manipulatives in the corners, thereby implying a rounded form in the center of the classroom. For them, round forms add symbolic value to the space. The centers or plazas of their pueblos take on a synthesizing and emanation function from which all things flow and to which all things return. Circular forms, pathways, open and closed space, and the use of the center of the classroom made sense, perhaps for all early or elementary classrooms.

Our experience was echoed at the Pine Hill School on the Navajo reservation in Arizona, the nation's first self-determined Native American School. There, architects assessed group preferences for fireplaces, roof lines, colors, and other architectural elements (*Albuquerque Journal* 1980). In general, the Navajos preferred polygonal or round shapes to rectangular shapes, which they associated with the Bureau of Indian Affairs schools. They emphatically stated that the buildings should not be connected because they wanted their children to experience nature, hot and cold, snow and sun. Contact with nature is a most important educational element for the Navajo.

This suggests that future classroom design, for this population and all peoples, should utilize space in a more symbolic way, congruent with the value system prized by a culture. Classrooms could take on a deep significance rather than being passive empty space.

Hence, in designing learning environments with diverse cultural groups, knowing how they symbolically perceive the environment and the things in it is important for making the appropriate inclusions or eliminations.

A CURRICULUM FOR ARCHITECTURE

As an adjunct to our work in learning environment design, George Vlastos and I created *Architecture and Children*, a curriculum and staff development program to teach architecture and design principles as well as drawing, model building, history, science, and math. The program also seeks to empower teachers and children to communicate visually with architects so they can help design the learning environments of the future.

In several instances this visual literacy program has spawned some excellent programs by teachers and children, who, given the tools for creative problem solving, have made valuable and expert input to new or retrofitted school and playground design.

By using architectural programming, middle school students at Riverside School in Spokane, Washington, saved their school $1,200 and obtained the playground they wanted. They first investigated the site and the adult choice of playground equipment, discovering that the intended premanufactured playground equipment was not developmentally appropriate for their needs. They then created a "landscape design for learning" that called for no equipment, and they

presented their ideas for the site to their principal. These students succeeded in influencing sensible decisions about the site, its age-appropriate function, and its future. They gained a sense of ownership over their environment, worked to improve it, and served their community—all as part of their everyday education.

A New School for Trout Lake

Architectural programming also played a significant role in the creation of a new school in Trout Lake, Washington. The community had defeated bond issues for a new school building for six years. Then the faculty of 15 and the student body of 150 K–12 students, using *Architecture and Children*, spent the year collecting data and writing about and drawing architectural concepts. Students in 3rd to 5th grade executed an environmental impact study of their playground to see whether it was suitable for use when the old school facilities were remodeled. They discovered that old septic tanks and drainage fields were producing "black water" in the spring and seepage from the drain fields. They then built models to depict their ideas for a new school.

The citizens of the area also met to discuss their preferences and, at the meeting, they viewed an exhibition of the children's architectural work. Prompted by the student messages that went home to families, they seemed more aware of the need for a new structure. Community members vehemently stated they didn't want just another school, but rather an intergenerational community center. One month later, the bond issue passed. Of special note is the level of indebtedness to which this small community committed itself—$4.83 per $100 of property assessment.

Now all parties look forward to an intergenerational community center, not just another cookie-cutter school. Their rural library will be a state-of-the-art system available for community use and connected by the latest technology to data banks around the state, the nation, and the world. The new cooking technology space will not only help children understand the benefits of good nutrition but will provide a space for community gourmet cooking classes. And as in any rural area, the gym will be an important gathering place. The superintendent hopes that rural music festivals will be as important as the sports events.

As the planning moves forward, the students have stayed involved. High school students are working with the U.S. Forest Service on an environmental impact study on the chosen site, and students will collaborate with the Soil Conservation Bureau to replant a diverted streambed. The architect will show students how to use computer-assisted design as he prepares the working drawings, and he will make his design disks available for community review of his progress. Students will also participate in landscaping and construction of play areas, observatories, and nature walks.

Besides learning about design and architecture, the students learned about the politics of pushing an idea. Their work helped to pull their community together, and the project gave the students in the district a sense of ownership in a real-life project to solve a community problem.

Restructuring in Stockton

Another example of how community involvement can create a new type of learning environment is taking place in the Lincoln Unified School District in Stockton, California. In recent years, the number of children from diverse cultural groups, including Cambodian, Vietnamese, and Hispanic, has increased in the district; 27 different languages are now spoken in district schools. To help meet the needs of these new students, a developer gave the district 40 acres on which to build a new high school and 120 acres along the San Joaquin River delta to use as an environmental study area.

Because the Lincoln School District believes their schools should be student-driven, the district curriculum coordinator, with help from architects and a consultant team, facilitated a series of think tanks with students, community members, and staff to conceptualize what the new school would be. As design consultants on the projects, we walked the empty site with the students who will learn there—talking, imagining, and sharing ideas and feelings. We built models with them, and we drove the students around Stockton on the school bus, learning what spaces they preferred.

This unique joint venture between developer and school district has picked up additional momentum because it coincides with several other restructuring efforts in the district. The district is striving for a more holistic and integrated curriculum, designed for many learning styles. District officials listened and heard students saying that schools needed to be more personal, learning needed to be more real, and students needed to participate in developing options so they feel a sense of belonging in the micro- and macro-community (MacKenzie 1992).

The participatory process of designing the new school has been a powerful learning experience, and the new high school will not be typical. It will be a community learning center that supplements already existing offerings in the district and the community. Students have inventoried community resources to assess the potential for real-life learning and work experiences. Physical resources will also be inventoried and become part of the environmental three-dimensional textbook. These resources include city planning, landscape and architectural design, and city transportation and communication networks. In addition, a working agricultural irrigation unit will be installed on the 40 acres.

Though not completed, the Lincoln project points the way for student participation in planning learning environments. In Stockton, the architectural programming process is no longer the sole domain of the school board or the administration; collaborative planning is everybody's business.

• • •

Schools are workplaces for children and teachers—the physical learning environments that support education. If we are to achieve the new visions of education, we must remodel current classrooms, design and build new schools and outdoor landscape laboratories, and rethink what "school" means in light of the changes we'd like to see. Perhaps schools won't look like schools, and classrooms won't look like classrooms. Perhaps there will be no classrooms. Perhaps we will be using the total community as a learning environment. As we begin building the schools we need for the 21st century, let's produce optimal—not minimal—learning environments, ones that act as teaching tools.

References

Council for Education Facility Planners International. (January 1995). "Education: Will Taxpayers See the Link Between Poor Schools and Poor Grades?" *Contract Design*, p. 64.

Gardner, H. (1983). *Frames of Mind: The Theory of Multiple Intelligences*. New York: Basic Books.

MacKenzie, T. (1992). "The Lincoln Plan." Unpublished manuscript, Lincoln Unified School District, Stockton, California.

Pena, W. (1987). *Problem Seeking*. Washington, D.C.: AIA Press.

Taylor, A. (1995). Architectural Program, Lincoln Unified School District, Stockton, Calif.

Taylor, A., and G. Vlastos. (1983). *School Zone: Learning Environments for Children*. 2nd ed. Albuquerque, N.M.: School Zone, Inc.

Taylor, A., and G. Vlastos. (1991). *Architecture and Children*. Seattle, Wash.: Architecture and Children Institute.

Taylor A., G. Vlastos, B. Wise, and J. Wise. (1989-92). *Head Start Classroom of the Future*. Preliminary Reports to Health and Human Services. Albuquerque: University of New Mexico.

WORDS BY KRISTA W. BARTON
PHOTOGRAPHS BY DEELYNN SMITH

STUDENTS IN WHEELCHAIRS HAVE PLENTY OF SPACE TO MANEUVER THROUGH THE
CAFETERIA LINES AT LARKSPUR MIDDLE SCHOOL. THE COUNTER HEIGHT ALLOWS STUDENTS
IN WHEELCHAIRS TO PROCEED THROUGH THE LINE JUST AS EVERYONE ELSE DOES.

OPENING DOORS FOR STUDENTS WITH DISABILITIES: A PHOTO ESSAY

Schools are spaces where children learn, live, and grow. Within these spaces, children need to become increasingly independent, to feel safe and comfortable, and to learn all they can. Children with disabilities, like other children, can accomplish these goals when their surroundings accommodate their needs. The photos in this chapter show modifications in buildings, classrooms, and athletic facilities that have made the school accessible to all students.

ACHIEVING INDEPENDENCE

"TIME FOR RECESS!" AN ANNOUNCEMENT CHILDREN LOVE TO HEAR. AT CORPORATE LANDING ELEMENTARY SCHOOL, ALL CHILDREN CAN PARTICIPATE, THANKS TO WHEELCHAIR-ACCESSIBLE PLAYGROUND EQUIPMENT. CHILDREN WITH DISABILITIES HAVE A LEVEL PLAYING FIELD HERE!

AT OCEAN LAKES HIGH SCHOOL, THIS STUDENT CAN "PHONE HOME"—OR ANYWHERE ELSE—DESPITE HIS HEARING IMPAIRMENT, USING A TELETYPEWRITER (TTY).

149
NUTRITION SCIENCE / CULINARY ARTS

AT OCEAN LAKES HIGH SCHOOL, IT'S EASY
TO IDENTIFY THE ROOM YOU'RE
LOOKING FOR. ALL SIGNS INCLUDE BRAILLE
FOR PERSONS WITH VISUAL IMPAIRMENTS.

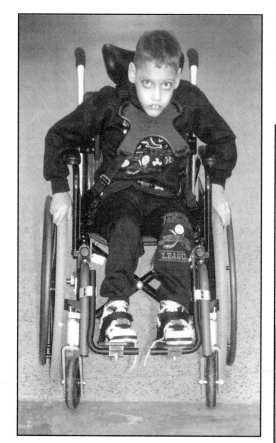

RAMPS LIKE THIS ONE ALLOW STUDENTS IN WHEELCHAIRS TO SAFELY TRAVEL BETWEEN THE WINGS OF PEMBROKE ELEMENTARY SCHOOL. A NONSLIP SURFACE PROVIDES EXTRA TRACTION.

EVEN A PERSON WITH A TEMPORARY DISABILITY APPRECIATES THE ACCOMMODATIONS AT OCEAN LAKES HIGH SCHOOL. THIS STUDENT WITH AN ARM INJURY HAS EASY ACCESS TO THE RESTROOM BECAUSE OF THE LEVER-STYLE DOOR HANDLE. LEVER DOOR HANDLES REQUIRE SIMPLER OPERATING MOVEMENTS THAN TRADITIONAL DOORKNOBS.

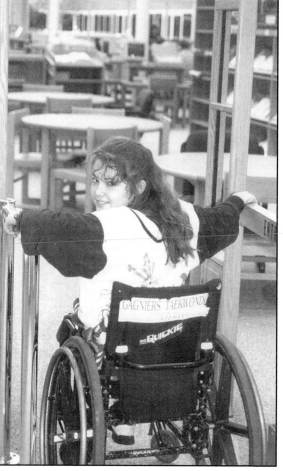

WHEN DESIGNING THE SECURITY ENTRANCE FOR THE LIBRARY AT OCEAN LAKES HIGH SCHOOL, THE ARCHITECTS KEPT IN MIND THE WIDTH OF THE LIGHTWEIGHT WHEELCHAIRS FAVORED BY YOUNG PEOPLE WITH DISABILITIES.

THIRSTY? GETTING A DRINK IS NOT A PROBLEM
FOR ERICA AT OCEAN LAKES HIGH SCHOOL.
THIS ACCESSIBLE WATER FOUNTAIN PERMITS HER
TO QUENCH HER THIRST WITHOUT ASSISTANCE.

FEELING SAFE AND COMFORTABLE

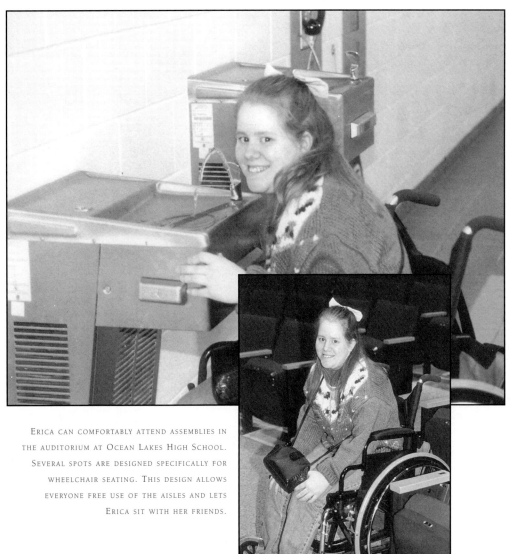

ERICA CAN COMFORTABLY ATTEND ASSEMBLIES IN
THE AUDITORIUM AT OCEAN LAKES HIGH SCHOOL.
SEVERAL SPOTS ARE DESIGNED SPECIFICALLY FOR
WHEELCHAIR SEATING. THIS DESIGN ALLOWS
EVERYONE FREE USE OF THE AISLES AND LETS
ERICA SIT WITH HER FRIENDS.

VISUAL FIRE ALARMS THAT BLINK LIKE STROBE
LIGHTS HAVE BEEN INSTALLED AT OCEAN LAKES HIGH
SCHOOL. STUDENTS WITH HEARING IMPAIRMENTS FEEL
MORE SECURE KNOWING THEY CAN SEE THE ALARM.

ACCOMMODATING PRESCHOOL CHILDREN IS EASY WITH
A FEW ADJUSTMENTS: A STOOL GIVES A LITTLE EXTRA
HEIGHT, AND THE LEVER-STYLE FAUCET IS EASY TO
OPERATE. NEXT TO THE SINK, A WIDE COUNTERTOP
IS AVAILABLE FOR DIAPER CHANGES, AND THE CABINET
PROVIDES SPACE TO STORE SUPPLIES.

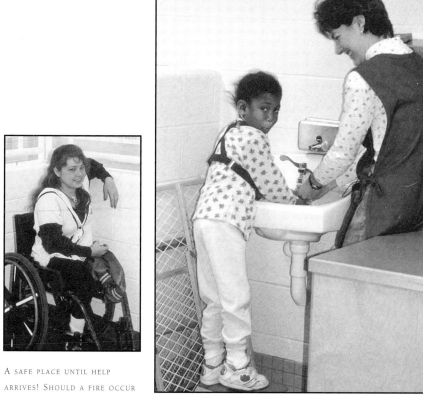

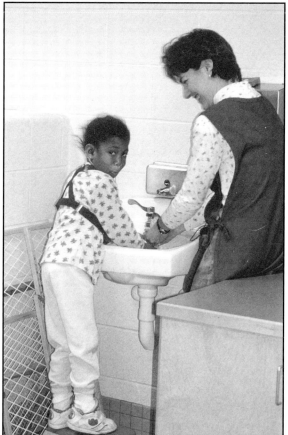

A SAFE PLACE UNTIL HELP
ARRIVES! SHOULD A FIRE OCCUR
AT OCEAN LAKES HIGH SCHOOL,
THIS PROTECTED LOCATION,
COMPLETE WITH FIRE WALL,
WILL KEEP STUDENTS WITH
DISABILITIES OUT OF CROWDS
WHILE THEY WAIT FOR HELP.

AT PEMBROKE ELEMENTARY SCHOOL, HANDRAILS
ARE INCLUDED ON BOTH SIDES OF THIS
RAMP FOR EXTRA SAFETY AND ASSISTANCE.

GAINING ACCESS TO LEARNING

AT CORPORATE LANDING ELEMENTARY SCHOOL, THE LATEST TECHNOLOGY IS AVAILABLE. THIS SPEECH TEACHER IS USING A COMPUTER WITH A SPEECH VIEWER TO TEACH SOUND PRODUCTION TO STUDENTS WHO HAVE HEARING IMPAIRMENTS. ALTHOUGH THE STUDENTS CAN'T HEAR THEMSELVES MAKE THE CORRECT SOUNDS, THEY CAN SEE THEIR SUCCESS IN THE VISUAL FEEDBACK ON THE SCREEN.

THANKS TO CLOSED CAPTIONING, STUDENTS WITH HEARING IMPAIRMENTS HAVE ACCESS TO EDUCATIONAL VIDEOS AT CORPORATE LANDING ELEMENTARY SCHOOL.

LORENA WORKS ON DOMESTIC LIVING SKILLS IN THIS WHEELCHAIR-ACCESSIBLE KITCHEN AT PEMBROKE ELEMENTARY SCHOOL. MINOR KITCHEN ACCOMMODATIONS, SUCH AS SUCTION CUPS ON THE BOTTOM OF PLATES AND VELCRO ON DISH TOWELS, ASSIST STUDENTS IN LEARNING.

A POPULAR ACTIVITY DURING P.E. IS JETMOBILING. THIS STUDENT IS DEVELOPING UPPER BODY STRENGTH WHILE HAVING FUN. THE PEMBROKE ELEMENTARY SCHOOL GYM WAS SPECIFICALLY DESIGNED TO MEET THE NEEDS OF CHILDREN WITH DISABILITIES. NOTE THE THERAPY MAT, MIRROR, AND BOLSTER IN THE BACKGROUND.

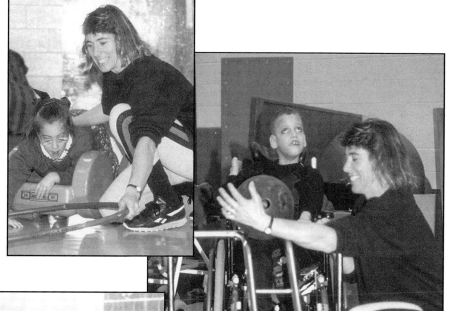

IN THIS P.E. CLASS AT PEMBROKE ELEMENTARY SCHOOL, THE ADAPTIVE PHYSICAL EDUCATION TEACHER HELPS A STUDENT IN A WHEELCHAIR JOIN IN A GAME OF BOWLING. WITH THIS SPECIALLY DESIGNED RAMP, EVEN A LIGHT TOUCH CAN RESULT IN A STRIKE!

AN ELEVATOR MAKES GETTING TO CLASS ON TIME EASY FOR KANSIS AT OCEAN LAKES HIGH SCHOOL. THE LESS TIME SPENT TRAVELING TO AND FROM CLASS, THE MORE TIME SPENT IN CLASS!

USING A SWITCH THAT REQUIRES ONLY THE LIGHTEST TOUCH, MARK IS INTERACTING WITH A COMPUTER PROGRAM. THE SUPINE STANDER THAT HE IS POSITIONED IN ALLOWS HIM GREATER PHYSICAL MOVEMENT THAN A WHEELCHAIR WOULD. THE COMPUTER MONITOR HAS BEEN RAISED TO MARK'S EYE LEVEL.

KANSIS CAN USE THE
COMPUTERS IN THE LIBRARY
BECAUSE THEY ARE ON
EASILY ACCESSIBLE DESKS.

STUDENTS AT LARKSPUR MIDDLE SCHOOL
HAVE FULL ACCESS TO TRACK AND OTHER
SPORTS EQUIPMENT. NOTICE THE WIDTH
OF THE LANES—ENOUGH TO ALLOW FOR
WHEELCHAIR MOVEMENT.

KANSIS CAN
PARTICIPATE
FULLY IN LAB
EXPERIMENTS
DURING
CHEMISTRY
CLASS, USING
THIS FULLY
ACCESSIBLE
PORTABLE
LAB TABLE.

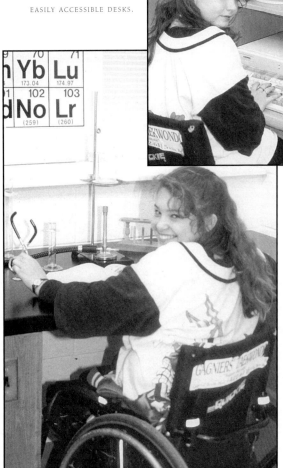

When a school facility accommodates all students' needs, everyone wins: teachers are pleased that students get to class on time, students are happy to sit with their friends during an assembly, and administrators and parents are relieved that safety issues are effectively handled.

Altering a building to meet the needs of all children provides an efficient, effective, humanistic environment for children to live and grow in. Accessibility within schools gives students with disabilities the opportunity to participate fully in life and learning. Independence, safety, comfort, and access to learning—these are what school is all about, for everyone.

A BUILDING IN POOR
REPAIR CONTRIBUTES TO THE
ATTITUDE AND DISCIPLINE
PROBLEMS AMONG STUDENTS,
WHICH IN TURN CONTRIBUTE
TO POOR PERFORMANCE
IN SCHOOLS.

—COPE (1989)

BUILDINGS MATTER: THE CONNECTIONS BETWEEN SCHOOL BUILDING CONDITIONS AND STUDENT ACHIEVEMENT IN WASHINGTON, D.C.

10

MAUREEN M. BERNER

The physical condition of the public schools in the District of Columbia is alarming. Problems range from missing toilet stall doors in restrooms to broken windows, nonfunctioning fire alarm systems, and entire buildings recommended for closing.

In 1989, the D.C. Committee on Public Education (COPE) surveyed conditions in the Washington, D.C., public school system and estimated the repair cost of deferred maintenance to be $150 million, with an additional $30 million needed for air conditioning. At that time, the system had 199 facilities that were, on average, 50 years old.

The report also identified problems in the management of repair requests. Between 1986–1989, of an estimated 21,295 work orders placed by the schools, only 3,559 were completed, with an average response time of 3 to 6 months. Interestingly enough, the first recommendation in the COPE report was to provide schools with soap/detergent, floor wax, light bulbs, and paper towels—amenities people usually take for granted.

The COPE report concluded that these conditions combine to convey the message that "what is going on inside [the schools] is not important, that the school system is uncaring, and that neglect is tolerated" (1989, p. 129). It went on to assert that "a building in poor repair contributes to the attitude and discipline problems among students, *which in turn contribute to poor performance in schools.* Hence, as a community, we must, at a minimum, provide our teachers and students with facilities that are decent and safe" [italics added].

 ## BUILDINGS MATTER

In 1990–91, I used Washington, D.C., as a case study[1] to examine the relationship between parental involvement and school building conditions and between building conditions and student achievement.

---

[1]The research for this study was completed in partial fulfillment of requirements for a master's degree in Public Policy at Georgetown University. The conclusions represent solely the views of the author. See Berner 1993 for a full description of the research design, methodology, and results of this study.

At that time, the D.C. school system was responsible for 191 educational facilities and enrolled about 83,000 students, a population that was approximately 90 percent black, 4 percent white, and 6 percent other minority (Asian, Native American, and Hispanic).

I hypothesized that the condition of public school buildings is (1) affected by parental involvement and (2) affects student achievement. I tested these hypotheses using regression models controlling for several variables: the type of school building (elementary, junior high, or high school), the PTA budget, the age of the school, racial makeup and mean income in the school's neighborhood, and school enrollment.

The results of the study revealed that greater parental involvement (as indicated by the size of the school's PTA budget) is associated with better physical conditions for school buildings. And physical condition is, in turn, statistically related to students' academic achievement. Schools were classified as poor, fair, or excellent. An improvement in physi-

OLDER BUILDINGS ARE OFTEN IN BETTER CONDITION THAN THOSE BUILT TO ACCOMMODATE THE BABY BOOM.

cal condition by one category, say, from poor to fair, was associated with a 5.5 point improvement in average academic achievement scores on standardized tests. For instance, if a school's condition were to move from poor to excellent, we could predict an increase of approximately 11 points in the school's average achievement scores.

During my study, I found that enrollment and building age also affect building condition, although the school's age was not as great an influence as one might expect. Older buildings are often in better condition than those built to accommodate the baby boom. Elementary schools tended to be in better condition than other schools. In addition, there was a positive correlation between enrollment and building condition—possibly because larger schools have more resources, financial and human, to deal with major repairs.

The study also showed that although enrollment has a positive correlation with building condition, it is negatively related to student achievement. As school enrollment goes up, average student achievement scores go down. An increase of 100 students could be expected to reduce a school's average achievement scores by 8.8 points.

Income and racial makeup were also found to influence achievement; schools in wealthier, more predominantly white areas were likely to have higher average achievement scores.

These results confirm the assertions of the various national reports that implore policymakers to address the basic condition of schools as a means of improving educational outcomes. One could, however, also see the effects of parental selection in these findings, as motivated parents could simply be avoiding schools they see deteriorating.

 ## A GOOD PLACE TO START

The costs of deferred maintenance of public school buildings extend beyond the expense of new boilers and alarm systems. The D.C. public school system needs more than $150 million just to bring buildings up to what is normally considered usable condition. Good infrastructure is at the base of quality education. For a society searching for ways to address the educational demands of the future, the building itself is a good place to start.

References

American Association of School Administrators, Council of Great City Schools, and the National School Boards Association. (1983). *The Maintenance Gap: Deferred Repair and Renovation in the Nation's Elementary and Secondary Schools.* Washington, D.C.: Authors.

Berner, M.M. (April 1993). "Building Conditions, Parental Involvement, and Student Achievement in the District of Columbia Public School System." *Urban Education* 28, 1: 6–29.

COPE. (1989). *Our Children, Our Future: Revitalizing the District of Columbia Public Schools.* Washington, D.C.: District of Columbia Committee on Public Education.

THE COST OF
OBSOLESCENCE IS
INCURRED THROUGH
LOST OPPORTUNITY AS
PEOPLE AND MATERIAL
ASSETS PERFORM LESS
PRODUCTIVELY THAN
THEY MIGHT.

WASTING OUR ASSETS: THE COSTS OF NEGLECTING THE NATION'S EDUCATION INFRASTRUCTURE

ANDREW C. LEMER

During the 1980s, the term "infrastructure" emerged from technical obscurity to become almost a household word. Concerns about neglect of the nation's highways, water supply systems, and sewers—the supporting foundations for much of the nation's economic and social activity—gave rise to dire warnings about "America in ruins," and a protracted national debate over appropriate levels of investment and subsequent maintenance. In much of this debate, schools and other public buildings, which provide services as vital to the nation's well-being as roads, water, and sewers, received meager notice. Yet the problems are similar, as are their sources; and the costs of their neglect are substantial.

FINANCIAL
LIMITATIONS
RENDER SOME
SCHOOL
DISTRICTS
"UNABLE TO
PROGRESS
WITH
REGARD TO
PRESENT-DAY
STANDARDS
AND CODES."

NEGLECTING EDUCATIONAL INFRASTRUCTURE

Unfortunately, cases of neglected educational infrastructure are easily found. Montgomery County, Maryland, a suburban center within the Washington, D.C., metropolitan area, is one of the nation's wealthiest local jurisdictions. The highly regarded quality of its schools is an important attraction for the county's substantial middle-class and wealthier residents. Nevertheless, like many of their colleagues around the nation, Montgomery County's elected officials, when faced with budget deficits during the early 1990s, cut school budgets. According to a newspaper report (*The Washington Post* 1991) at the time, the county hoped to save nearly $1.8 million by reducing a variety of educational services and activities, more than 40 percent of these "savings" to be realized by performing only emergency maintenance and changing building management policy to use less heating or cooling in the schools.

Montgomery County's situation is remarkable only because of the jurisdiction's wealth and the apparent importance of its schools to its taxpayers. The use of school facilities as a means for cutting government costs is unfortunately common and widespread. A national survey (Agron 1993) found that average spending for maintenance and operations by school districts nationwide declined nearly 16 percent during the 1992–93 school year from the previous year. A study by the Education Writers Association (1989) judged that the physical condition of one of every four American school buildings was inadequate. Of these, just over 60 percent were inadequate because of needs for maintenance or major repairs.

And the problem is not new. In a 1990 study of the state of Washington's schools (personal communication 1991) done by its Division of School Facilities and Organization, the state superintendent of public instruction found that total maintenance spending, measured in constant dollars (that is, adjusted for inflation's impact), had declined each year from 1981 through 1988. During the same period, student enrollment increased by 12,000 and the physical plant was expanded by some 12 million square feet statewide.

But "savings" are made not only by reducing maintenance spending. Forty-three percent of the schools found to be inadequate by the Education Writers Association (1989) were termed obsolete, 42 percent had environmental hazards, and 13 percent were structurally unsound. Many schools had multiple problems.

The 1990 Ohio Public School Facility Survey (Ohio Department of Education 1990) found that electrical systems were satisfactory in only about half of that state's schools. Only about one-fourth had satisfactory plumbing, and fewer than one in five had acceptable heating systems. The state's superintendent of public instruction noted the financial limitations that rendered some school districts "unable to progress with regard to present-day standards and codes." The survey team estimated that more than $10 billion would be needed to bring the state's approximately 3,600 elementary, middle and junior high, and high schools up to good working condition.

 THE COSTS OF
"SAVINGS"

As Ohio's experience demonstrates, the "savings" achieved by neglecting educational facilities are false. Neglecting maintenance, for a start, simply defers the cost and creates a backlog of needed work that, in all likelihood, will increase the cost as well as shift the burden to future taxpayers. In this sense, maintenance deferral is a form of embezzlement of future taxpayers' funds, often perpetrated for political expediency.

But the costs go beyond the maintenance backlog. Poor conditions represent reduced service levels for students and teachers. These reduced service levels, in turn, reduce the effectiveness of the entire educational program. Such ineffective spending is a second source of cost that offsets "savings."

Over the longer term, the progressive obsolescence of schools is a third factor offsetting "savings." New knowledge about learning, new technologies, changes in culture, and changes in the role of the schoolhouse in the community create new demands that older school buildings are poorly suited to meet. The cost of obsolescence is incurred through lost opportunity as people and material assets perform less productively than they might.

These three sources of cost—deferred maintenance, reduced service levels, and obsolescence—are not well documented and are frequently overlooked, but they are nevertheless real and often substantial.

The Costs of Deferred Maintenance

Most people probably understand that buildings require some regular care and maintenance and that schools may be more likely to need such care than many other types of buildings. Yet national studies (Committee on Advanced Maintenance Concepts for Buildings 1990) have found that underfunding of maintenance and repair (M&R) is a widespread and persistent problem for public buildings. Experts propose that annual spending for normal maintenance (excluding correction of deficiencies created by prior neglect or catastrophes) should be budgeted, on average and for large groups of buildings, at 2 to 4 percent of current replacement value, but statistics for schools show this funding is seldom available.

The 1989 Education Writers' Association study cited states' estimates that $41 billion was needed to correct deficiencies in the nation's more than 88,000 public schools, about 10 percent of their estimated current replacement value. Ohio's 1990 survey placed the cost of needed repair and rebuilding (excluding needed additions) of

STUDENTS, WHO
DESIRE AND
DESERVE
ORDER, BEAUTY,
AND SAFE
SURROUNDINGS,
POINT OUT
BATHROOMS
FILTHY BECAUSE
OF WATER-
DAMAGED
FLOORS AND
FIXTURES.

its schools at more than $8 billion. These are added costs, beyond those for normal maintenance, that might have been avoided had normal maintenance been properly carried out.

The evidence of such neglect and underfunding is often readily apparent. In one large city school district, for example, budgets were adequate to paint classrooms only once every 100 years and to replace floor coverings once every 50 years (Corcoran, Walker, and White 1988). Short of installing marble or other comparably durable materials on floors and walls, standard management practice and current technology can deliver, at most, 10 years of satisfactory service without replacement of these hard-used building components—and neglect of regular maintenance can reduce the service life substantially.

New York City's schools became notorious early in the 1993–94 school year because faulty inspections for asbestos in more than 1,000 buildings delayed school openings. Nationally syndicated columnist George Will (1993) cited the *New Yorker* magazine's report of city government estimates that 544,000 of the 800,000 buildings in the city contained asbestos. In about 90 percent of those, building decay caused the exposure of the asbestos.

Similarly, a California school was closed when paint allowed to deteriorate until it began flaking was found to be lead-based (Little Hoover Commission 1992). Regardless of the scientific debate over the dangers of asbestos or lead, public concern makes the cost of this neglect huge. And as courts end school district immunity to tort liability actions (for example, Illinois Supreme Court, *Molitor v. Kaneland* 1959, cited by Sharp 1992), these huge costs grow in size and effect.

The Costs of Reduced Service Levels

Of course, those responsible for school budget and maintenance deferral decisions will say that the funds are simply not there and the "savings" must be made. But even if the direct costs of deferral were not so substantial, there are devastating costs imposed on school users, the students and their teachers. These costs are paid in lost capacity for learning and teaching and in the message delivered that education is not important.

Interviews within classrooms are most telling (*Voices from the Inside* 1992). Staff and students repeatedly complain about their physical environment: "It's so muggy here today that I was almost sick at lunch. . . . How many executives in business sit in rooms like that? Show me one." Despite custodial efforts, students, who desire and deserve order, beauty, and decent, safe surroundings, point out bathrooms filthy because of water-damaged floors and fixtures.

The likely link between facilities and educational performance or outcome has also long been recognized. Urban school officials in the early decades of this century endorsed new furnaces for control of classroom temperatures and air currents for upgrading student achievement and deportment (Rose and Clark 1979). An advertisement placed in a 1919 issue of Denver's Chamber of Commerce weekly by members of the School Bond Election Committee claimed "Children go each day to crowded schools with badly ventilated . . . rooms, and . . . too many are ill every year from polluted air—air you'd not tolerate in your offices" (reproduced in Rose and Clark 1979).

The complexity of the linkage has obstructed its measurement. One review of 232 separate research studies concluded that definite findings were difficult to ascertain (Earthman 1986). Nevertheless, one recent study of schools in Washington, D.C., showed a statistically significant relationship between achievement test scores and the physical conditions of school buildings (Berner 1993). An increase of nearly 11 points in average test scores could be expected to accompany an improvement of conditions from "poor" to "excellent" (Berner 1993) (see Chapter 10 of this book). Deteriorated school building conditions can thus reduce the effectiveness of the entire program of educational spending, a potentially large cost for small "savings."

The Costs of Obsolescence

Studies of school conditions invariably cite obsolescence, a result of changes in the requirements or expectations a building is to fulfill, as a problem (Iselin and Lemer 1993). Neglect of maintenance hastens obsolescence. In the absence of proper maintenance, building service conditions decline more rapidly and fall below increasing requirements that much sooner. As with the costs of reduced service levels, the costs of obsolescence are difficult to isolate and measure.

The service life of a building and its interior components, normally expected to be in the range of 10 to 30 years, can be reduced by several years if the building does not receive routine maintenance. For a school building that would cost $10 million to build today, that loss could represent an equivalent cost of some $1 to $2 million, a cost imposed on those who either lose the use of the facility or are forced prematurely to rebuild it.

COMMITTING TO THE COSTS

Cases such as those reviewed here demonstrate the size and severity of the costs of neglect of our education infrastructure. They may be difficult to measure, but they eventually must be paid, typically by students and teachers whose capacities to learn and teach are impaired; by today's parents and other taxpayers whose investment in education is being eaten away; and by those in the future who must repair and rebuild schools, sooner and at higher costs than should be the case.

The likelihood that costs will be borne by others is a key to why neglect is possible. Faced with competing demands for limited funds and the immediacy of many of these demands—for example, programs for social welfare and criminal justice as well as teachers' salaries and student activities—it is small wonder that school buildings are neglected. The deterioration is slow to occur and difficult to see. And the institutional biases against maintenance are substantial. The work of maintenance and rehabilitation is less appealing to politicians and administrators who may gain positive notice when they cut the ribbons for new buildings, and to architects and engineers who understandably prefer to do new things. The buildings themselves have no vote.

The problems are similar for all types of infrastructure and in all places. The World Bank's (1989) assessment of the long-term prospects for Sub-Saharan Africa's development refers to the "pernicious" impact of infrastructure maintenance fund diversions, and concludes that only by earmarking the funds—restricting the administrators' and politicians' ability to spend the funds for anything other than maintenance—can the situation be changed. Such earmarking is considered undesirable by most economists because it may prevent efficient resource allocation. For school buildings and other elements of the infrastructure, that risk seems unavoidably necessary. The procedures of public sector budgeting and spending simply lack adequate discipline for reliable maintenance of these major public assets.

One form of earmarking that has gained some popularity among charitable foundations supporting educational facilities development is the maintenance trust. When a new building is constructed, funds are placed into a trust or other reserve fund that will in future years yield income adequate for the building's maintenance. Such a strategy represents a major increase in the capital required at the time of building construction, but also a solid commitment to the long-term costs of building ownership. Such long-term commitment is needed to get the most from school buildings and other parts of the public infrastructure.

• • •

School buildings, once the symbol of a community's determination to secure a better future, have been neglected in discussions of education policy as well as in their physical upkeep. Failing to maintain these elements of the nation's infrastructure has lasting costs that far exceed the short-term savings often used to justify the neglect.

References

Agron, J. (April 1993). "A Drop in the Bucket. 22nd Annual M&O Cost Study." *American School and University* 65, 8: 28–32.

Berner, M.M. (April 1993). "Building Conditions, Parental Involvement, and Student Achievement in the District of Columbia Public School System." *Urban Education* 28, 1: 6–29.

Committee on Advanced Maintenance Concepts for Buildings. (1990). *Committing to the Cost of Ownership: Maintenance and Repair of Public Buildings.* Washington, D.C.: National Academy Press.

Corcoran, T.B., L.J. Walker, and J.L. White. (1988). *Working in Urban Schools*. Washington, D.C.: Institute for Educational Leadership.

Earthman, G. (1986). "Research Needs in the Field of Educational Facility Planning." Paper presented at the Edusystems 2000 International Congress on Educational Facilities, Values, and Contents in Jerusalem. [ERIC Document Reproduction Services (no. ED 283 301)].

Education Writers Association. (1989). *Wolves at the Schoolhouse Door: An Investigation of the Condition of Public School Buildings*. Washington, D.C.: Education Writers Association.

Iselin, D.G., and A.C. Lemer, eds. (1993). *The Fourth Dimension in Building: Strategies for Minimizing Obsolescence*. Washington, D.C.: National Academy Press, Building Research Board.

Little Hoover Commission. (1992). *No Room for Johnny: A New Approach to the School Facilities Crisis*. Sacramento, Calif.: Commission on California State Government Organization and Economy.

Ohio Department of Education. (November 1990). "1990 Ohio Public School Facility Survey." Columbus, Ohio: Ohio Department of Education.

Sharp, W.L. (1992). "Preventive Maintenance: Toward an Extended Concept." *CEFPI's Educational Facility Planner* 30, 4: 11–13.

State of Washington. Author's personal communication with personnel on the staff of the Superintendent of Public Instruction, April 1991.

Rose, M.H., and J.G. Clark. (May 1979). "Heat, Light, and Power: Energy Choices in Kansas City, Witchita, and Denver, 1900–1935." *Journal of Urban History* 5, 3: 340–364.

Voices from the Inside: A Report on Schooling from Inside the Classroom. (1992). Claremont, Calif.: The Institute for Education in Transformation at the Claremont Graduate School.

The Washington Post, Thursday, November 28, 1991, p. B11.

Will, G.F. (September 16, 1993). "Public School Shambles." *The Washington Post*, sec. A, p. 29.

The World Bank. (1989). *Sub-Saharan Africa: From Crisis to Sustainable Development*. Washington, D.C.: The World Bank.

RESOURCES

 READING LIST

Technical Guides

Comprehensive Bibliography on Child Care and Preschool Design, 1994, compiled by Gary T. Moore, Center for Architecture and Urban Planning Research, University of Wisconsin-Milwaukee, P.O. Box 413, Milwaukee, WI 53201, published simultaneously with American Institute of Architects, 1735 New York Ave., N.W., Washington, DC 20006. Bibliographic entries include research, design examples, and other published materials.

Educational Facilities for the 21st Century: Research, Analysis, and Design Patterns, 1994, by Gary T. Moore and Jeffery A. Lackney, Center for Architecture and Urban Planning Research, University of Wisconsin-Milwaukee, P.O. Box 413, Milwaukee, WI 53201. Presents 27 design patterns that better support educational achievement. A comprehensive report of the study on which Chapter 2 of this book is based.

Educational Facilities: The Impact and Role of the Physical Environment of the School on Teaching, Learning, and Educational Outcomes, 1992, by Jeffery A. Lackney, Center for Architecture and Urban Planning Research, University of Wisconsin-Milwaukee, P.O. Box 413, Milwaukee, WI 53201. Views the physical environment of the school as an integral part of the overall context for learning. Presents several models and frameworks for understanding facilities before planning begins.

Guide for Planning Educational Facilities, 1995, edited by Deborah P. Moore, The Council of Educational Facility Planners, International, 8687 E. Via de Ventura, Suite 311, Scottsdale, AZ 85258. A contemporary, A–Z resource for the planning, design, and construction of educational facilities.

Guide for School Facility Appraisal, 1992, by Harold L. Hawkins and H. Edward Lilley for The Council of Educational Facility Planners International. Divides appraisal criteria into six chapters and discusses how to use the sets of criteria for various purposes such as examining the need for renovation or for new facilities. Easy to use and helpful for building principals as well as facilities planners and administrators responsible for construction projects.

Planning for Technology: A Guidebook for School Administrators, 1993, by Dan Lumley and Gerald D. Bailey, Scholastic, Inc. A comprehensive yet easy-to-follow handbook, featuring a six-step planning process, complete with sample plans and transparencies.

Publications in Architecture and Urban Planning Research, 1995, by the
Center for Architecture and Urban Planning Research, University
of Wisconsin-Milwaukee, P.O. Box 413, Milwaukee, WI 53201.

Articles

"America's Best Buildings," by David C. Anderson, with photographs by
Lizzie Himmel, *The New York Times Magazine*, February 20, 1994.
Comparisons between school buildings and prisons; for example,
a photograph of South Boston High School, built in 1901 and
most recently expanded in 1940, with Boston's Suffolk County
Jail, opened in 1990.

"Does Equal Access Have to Be Ugly Access?" by Robert Campbell, *The
Boston Sunday Globe*, December 22, 1991. Appeals for careful
appraisal of the effects of the Americans with Disabilities Act on
the built environment.

"Education in Decay," *U.S. News & World Report*, September 12, 1994.
Describes the nation's crumbling schools in graphic terms, with
examples from the District of Columbia, New Orleans, and
Cincinnati. Gives figures for what is needed nationwide and men-
tions Senator Carol Moseley-Braun's (D-IL) bill to help fix schools.

"Fire-Code Violations Seen Placing Schools, Students in Jeopardy," by
Peter Schmidt, *Education Week*, June 8, 1994. Describes widespread fire-code violations in the nation's schools.

"Publications and Papers on Children and the Designed Environment,"
1995, by the Children's Environments Research and Design
Group, Center for Architecture and Urban Planning Research,
University of Wisconsin-Milwaukee, P.O. Box 413, Milwaukee,
WI 53201.

"Renovation Restores the Elegance of a Turn-of-the-Century Urban High
School," by Marilee C. Rist, *American School Board Journal*,

November 1990. Brief case study with photographs of successful
modernization with classroom addition at Maury High School,
built in 1911 in Norfolk, Virginia.

"School-Building Inventory Finds 1 in 8 Inadequate," by Peter Schmidt,
Education Week, November 27, 1991. Reports findings from a
survey (*Schoolhouse in the Red*) conducted by the American
Association of School Administrators in more than 15,000 school
districts nationwide.

Books

*Children, Learning & School Design: A First National Invitational Conference
for Architects and Educators*, 1992, edited by Elizabeth Hebert and
Anne Meek. Available from the Office of the Superintendent,
Winnetka Public Schools, Winnetka, IL 60093.

*The Geography of Nowhere: The Rise and Decline of America's Manmade
Landscape*, 1993, by James Howard Kunstler, Simon & Schuster.
A scathing critique of America's bad habits in architecture.

The Poetics of Space, 1969, by Gaston Bachelard, Beacon Press, Boston.
Philosophical and poetic ideas about human beings' responses to
and relationships with homes and their interiors.

*The Power of Place: How Our Surroundings Shape Our Thoughts, Emotions,
and Actions*, 1993, by Winifred Gallagher, Poseidon Press. Sets
aside the "false dichotomy" between biological and environmental
effects on human behavior; examines the effects of light, tempera-
ture, jet travel, a "change of scene," altitude, urbanization, and
other factors on how humans act and feel. Examples of settings
investigated include the womb, Alaska, wilderness, mountains,
and cities.

School Facilities: Condition of America's Schools. GAO Report B-259307.
United States General Accounting Office, Health, Education, and
Human Services Division, Washington, DC 20548. A well-written

and concise update based on a 1994 nationwide study, with tables, photos, and sample questionnaire.

Tomorrow's Learning Environment, by Franklin Hill, 1988, National School Boards Association, 1680 Duke Street, Alexandria, VA 22314. A useful guide for building and renovating schools, especially for incorporating technology into plans, not at all out-of-date for most districts. Includes specific suggestions for media centers, a prototype elementary classroom, middle school electronic neighborhoods, and science facilities. Also offers school district self-evaluation for facilitates and technology. Chapter 5 is a case study describing the design work for Dr. Phillips High School in Orange County, Florida, illustrating collaborative planning with industry for improved technology use. Annotated bibliography provides many excellent sources.

Schoolhouse in the Red, American Association of School Administrators, 1801 North Moore Street, Arlington, VA 22209. A 40-page summary of the findings of a 1991 survey and the proceedings of a 1992 conference regarding the condition of school facilities. Includes data and recommendations on maintenance, indoor air quality, energy, and efficiency. Provides a School Facility Evaluation Form for use by administrators, parents, and community. Practical and helpful.

School Ways: The Planning and Design of America's Schools, by Ben Graves, a 1993 Architectural Record/McGraw-Hill Co-publication. More than 200 pages of useful information and both black-and-white and color illustrations to show hundreds of school designs.

Wolves at the Schoolhouse Door: An Investigation of the Condition of Public School Buildings, 1989, by the Education Writers Association, 1001 Connecticut Ave. NW #310, Washington, DC 20036. 64-page report outlining the alarming status of America's schools, funding efforts, maintenance and training needs, and more.

ORGANIZATIONS AND OFFICES

American Association of School Administrators
1801 N. Moore St.
Arlington, VA 22209
703/528-0700

American Institute of Architects
1735 New York Avenue, N.W.
Washington, DC 20006
202/626-7300

The Council of Educational Facility Planners, International
8687 E. Via de Ventura, Suite 311
Scottsdale, AZ 85258–3347
602/948-2337 Fax: 602/948-4420

Creative Learning Systems Technology Lab 2000™/the Smart Lab™
16510 Via Esprillo
San Diego, CA 92127-1708
1-800-458-2880

National School Boards Association
1680 Duke Street
Alexandria, VA 22314
1-800-706-6722

Resource Systems, Computer and Custom Furniture for the
  Educational Environment
12972 Stamford Court
Livonia, MI 48150
1-800-637-2250